Like a Mighty Stream

Like a Mighty Stream

The March on Washington, August 28, 1963

by Patrik Henry Bass

RUNNING PRESS

PHILADELPHIA · LONDON

9 8 7 6 5 4 3 2 1
Digit on the right indicates the number of this printing

Library of Congress Cataloging-in-Publication Number 2002102856

ISBN 0-7624-1292-5

Photo Research by Leah Rudolfo
Additional photo research by Susan Oyama
Cover Design by Whitney Cookman
Cover Photograph: ©Flip Schulke/CORBIS
Front cover inset, spine and back cover: AP/Wide World Photos
Interior design by Bill Jones
Edited by Jeanine Rosen
Typography: Minion

This book may be ordered by mail from the publisher.
Please include $2.50 for postage and handling.
But try your bookstore first!

Running Press Book Publishers
125 South Twenty-second Street
Philadelphia, Pennsylvania 19103-4399

Visit us on the web!
www.runningpress.com

This young man was one of 250,000 who woke up on August 28, 1963 with his mind set on freedom.

CONTENTS

ACKNOWLEDGMENTS

*This book is humbly and sincerely dedicated
to the men, women and children who made
the journey to Washington on August 28, 1963.
Thank you for taking a stand and paving the way.*

My deep appreciation to everyone who gave me their time and shared their stories for this book: Evelyn Cunningham, Bob Zellner, Beverly Alston, Ed Bradley, Jr., Culie Vick and John Marshall Stevenson Kilimanjaro, Nan Grogan Orrock, Vertamae Grosvenor, and Reverend Abraham Woods. I owe so much to my parents Charles and Sarah Louise Bass, siblings Regina, Gregory, and Roderick Bass, and nieces KaTonya and Katrina for their prayers and patience. This book would not have been possible without my photo editor Leah Rudolfo and exquisite editors Janice K. Bryant and Jeanine Rosen, who gave the project their much needed attention. Thank you, Adreinne Waheed, for coming through the first time around. Mary Ann Smith-Janas, thank you for heeding my SOS. Thanks to Buz Teacher, Carlo DeVito, Jennifer Worick, Deborah Grandinetti, John Whalen, Sam Caggiula, and everyone at Running Press for the continued support. A special thank you to Bill Jones and Susan Oyama for going the extra mile. Thank you to everyone at Essence Communications Partners. Susan L. Taylor, thanks for the words of wisdom and encouragement. Imani Powell, thanks for holding everything down; Tamara Jeffries, thanks for lifting me up, and the swans (you know who you are) in F&B for sharing the nonstop laughter and love. Thank you to my publicist and friend Vanesse Lloyd-Sgmbati for spreading the word and keeping it real. God has blessed me with an incredible group of friends: Angela Spears, Pauline Barfield, Samuel Reed, Jr., Jane Best, Daren Kerr, Kent Davis, Mika Ono, Andrea Everett, Ursula Brown Robinson, Ylonda Gault-Caviness, Antoinette

L. Dalton, Bonnie Marshall, Lynn Whitfield, and Anne Woodward—who give me unconditional support. Robin Stone, you inspire me with your integrity and keen insight. Monique Greenwood—let me be clear about this: you are amazing! Finally, to my agent and dear friend Marie Brown, who attended the March; thank you for providing endless supplies of laughs, hugs, tough love, common sense, and gumbo, and of course, your incredible invitation to Manhattan Country School's 35th Anniversary, which helped get things on track.

A group of students, one of hundreds of groups that attended the March on Washington, gathers on the lawn.

INTRODUCTION

On August 28, 1963, more than 250,000 people—black and white, young and old, privileged and poor, and from every region of the country—converged on Washington, D.C. to demonstrate their support for the passage of a historic civil rights bill. Nearly forty years have passed since then, yet the March on Washington for Jobs and Freedom remains one of the most significant public demonstrations of the twentieth century—one that continues to have an impact today.

When I was first approached to write this book last fall, shortly after I completed *In Our Own Image: Treasured African American Traditions, Journeys and Icons,* with Karen Pugh, I was hesitant. There were already so many wonderful books on the Civil Rights Movement that incorporated the March on Washington, mainly Taylor Branch's *Parting the Waters,* Thomas Gentile's *The March on Washington,* David J. Garrow's *Bearing the Cross,* John Lewis' *Walking with the Wind,* and Diane McWhorter's Pulitzer Prize-winning *Carry Me Home.* I asked myself: Is there a need for another book on this subject?

I asked family, friends, and colleagues if they remembered the day or the year of the March on Washington. Only one answered correctly, and she had attended the March.

Again, I asked myself: *Is there a need for another book on this subject?*

This time, the answer was an unequivocal yes.

There have been other protest marches in Washington—most notably World War I veterans, and suffragettes at the dawn of the last century, and the Million Man and Mom Marches at the close of the century—yet no event has captured the world's attention, or transformed a nation, quite like the 1963 gathering.

Like a Mighty Stream is a retrospective documentation of the events that led to the March. The book zeroes in on the leaders who made it happen, and explores the impact it had on the people who attended. It illuminates one of the most intense moments of the Civil Rights Movement.

It is an incredible story. It is the story of dreams fulfilled and prayers answered. It is a story of great hope and patience, faith and fate. It is an epic story of standing firm in one's convictions against overwhelming odds. It is a story of American character and conviction. And it is ultimately a story about freedom.

The Civil Rights Movement was more than a cause—it was an American revolution fomented by ordinary men, women, and children, many of whom risked or gave their lives so that others might know freedom. While I was looking at images for *In Our Own Image*, it was not uncommon for me to come across photographs from the civil rights struggle that would leave me numb: a cowering black woman shopper being attacked with a baseball bat; the listless, burned, and bruised limbs of black men hanging from magnolia trees; rivulets of blood running down the faces of black reporters covering the Little Rock, Arkansas, desegregation; and fragile and sturdy bodies being trampled by troopers at the Edmund Pettus Bridge in Selma, Alabama.

Confronted with these images, some people turn the page or look the other way. Back then, as today, there were more trivial matters to keep people occupied. In 1963, people turned the dial to watch *The Andy Griffith Show* and *My Favorite Martian*. They switched radio stations from topical news to listen to "She Loves You" by The Beatles and "It's My Party" by Lesley Gore. Teenagers parked their Chevy Impalas at drive-ins to see Alfred Hitchcock's *The Birds* and *Jason and the Argonauts*, visually venturing into worlds far from their own. Yet at the same time, the Civil Rights Movement was at full throttle with hundreds participating in marches, protests, freedom rides, sit-ins, rallies, and voter registration drives.

While I am hopeful that future generations will acknowledge the incredible bravery of civil rights protesters, I know that today many of us continue to turn away. We point to individuals who excel in politics, entertainment, finance, athletics, and science, and suggest that things in some areas have changed for the better. In many ways they have. Yet there is still much work to be done.

Like most Americans, I knew that the March on Washington was the site of Martin Luther King, Jr.'s "I Have a Dream" speech. I was also aware that the March drew a massive crowd. I knew that it was a peaceful demonstration held in the summer. Much of what I knew I stumbled upon accidentally, while reading various biographies and narrative nonfiction, or watching an episode of *The Cosby Show* or the documentary *Eyes on the Prize.*

The March on Washington has now become a mythic event. We see nameless faces, gathered around the Reflecting Pool, carrying banners proclaiming, "I Am A Man" or "We Demand Jobs Now!" Without context, the March appeared to have been a joyful revival, a mammoth picnic in Washington, D.C., where everyone held hands and looked upward, joyously, to a brighter day. But the March on Washington was something more. It was the first signal that the Civil Rights Movement was a people's movement. It was the first time that Americans from all regions of the country came together to support one cause: the eventual passage of the Civil Rights Act of 1964. Although it was a multiracial, multidenominational march, far more blacks than whites attended it. All classes were represented, but there was a strong representation of the black working class. Although women had been practically silent on the podium, with the notable exceptions of Daisy Bates, Mahalia Jackson, and Marian Anderson, they were there in large numbers, supporting husbands, sons, and friends, representing civic organizations. Many celebrities—Paul Newman, Charlton Heston, Josephine Baker—went to Washington for the day, but no one received star treatment. It was that kind of march. And while King's "I Have a Dream" speech is remembered as one of the greatest speeches of the twentieth century, if not the greatest, labor leader Walter Reuther and Student Nonviolent Coordinating Committee Chairman John Lewis were among several others who gave rousing speeches.

The March had been a lifelong dream of A. Philip Randolph, leader of the Brotherhood of Sleeping Car Porters. He was involved in the plans for a similar march in 1941, but that initiative was ultimately abandoned. One of the remarkable truths to emerge from that day—and one of its chief lessons—is that the March succeeded because it was all-inclusive. For the first time, seasoned civil rights professionals from such organizations as the National Association for the Advancement of Colored People and the Urban League worked in concert with younger groups like the Southern Christian Leadership Conference (SCLC) and the Student Nonviolent Coordinating Committee (SNCC) as well as labor and religious groups. Yes, they had the usual disagreements, rivalries, and jockeying for position, but they were filled with a mutual respect for the mission: passage of the historic civil rights bill to end legal segregation.

One of the many delights in writing this book has been my chance encounters with some of the greatest personalities of the past century through newspaper clippings, speeches, in microform, and through letters. I am attracted to epic, cinematic stories, and the March on Washington was not only a first-rate production, but also had a dream cast: Asa Philip Randolph, the genteel giant, using wit and wisdom to keep his dream alive; the prickly and opinionated Roy Wilkins; Dr. Martin Luther King, Jr., the heir apparent and the people's choice; John F. Kennedy, the charismatic President, who slowly realizes that despite his considerable political gifts he couldn't control the tidal wave of change. There are dependable supporting players: John Lewis, whose integrity is as dear to him as the movement itself; Bayard Rustin, flawed dreamer and visionary, a man willing to remain in the background to keep his ideals in the forefront; and Anna Arnold Hedgeman, in many ways the conscience of the March; The clear antagonists: George Wallace and Bull Connor who represent racism at its most vicious; and many politicians who resisted voting for the bill for fear of losing votes from their constituents. It also had a cast of thousands—people of every age, race and religion, traveling miles to make their presence known on August 28, 1963.

The book is a look back—not just at 1963, but 1863 and 1941 as well. On January 1, 1863, President Abraham Lincoln signed the Emancipation Proclamation, which abolished slavery, but didn't free a single slave. The March on Washington occurred in the centennial year of the Emancipation Proclamation. The descendants of the enslaved had waited patiently for over a hundred years to enjoy the freedoms that other Americans knew as a birthright.

In 1941, A. Philip Randolph announced that 10,000 Negroes would march on Washington to denounce racism in defense industry hiring. After President Franklin D. Roosevelt issued an Executive Order to ban the practice, the black community's expectations of equality in America rose steadily. Yet, freedom was doled out on a piecemeal basis to the black community. For every step forward, there was resistance. And there was nowhere for blacks to turn except local, state, and federal courts. With the election of President John F. Kennedy in 1960, many black folks believed that the remnants of Jim Crow would be swept away by national legislation that would protect all Americans and honor the true principles on which this country was founded.

The March on Washington was a rallying cry against centuries of racial inequities in America. From enslavement to the Emancipation Proclamation, the New Deal to the New Frontier, America's black population was subjected to second-class status in employment, education, housing, and the political process. Despite a long-standing tradition of patriotism, from the American Revolutionary War through World War II, black veterans—their families and their descendants— were denied freedoms that they'd help secure for their fellow Americans.

During the postwar rebuilding of the United States of America, while black folks could see substantial progress—the victorious

Brown vs. The Board of Education decision in 1954, followed by the Montgomery bus boycotts, and the founding of the innovative civil rights groups the SCLC and the SNCC—they could feel the frustration over the lack of legislation that would end what was tantamount to American apartheid, rampant in the South, but evident throughout the rest of the country as well.

The frustrations were about major issues—employment, education, voting, and housing—and the impact of what not having access to these quintessential American principles and rights does to the psyche and the soul. What is its residual impact on those who are denied these things, and on those who are denying them?

These acts leave wounds. Whether accidental or intentional, these wounds will not go away unless they are given time to heal. These wounds need care and attention.

After more than 240 years, the damage on the collective soul of the black community *finally* received attention during President Lyndon Johnson's Great Society programs, the passage of the Civil Rights Act of 1964, the Voting Rights Act of 1965, and the Housing Rights Act of 1968.

In this book, there are remarkable individuals who bear witness to their memories of the March. It seemed vital to include eyewitness accounts. Some of the people here are prominent figures, watched and listened to by millions. Others are everyday folk, living their lives on a smaller scale, blending perfectly into the landscape. Their memories of August 28, 1963, differ widely. Some recall the day as one of the hottest of their lives; others thought it was a mild summer day. There are varying accounts of how many people they felt were at the March. There are differences over who actually attended the March—were there more men than women, and just as many whites as blacks? And there are differences about the progress that has been made over the past four decades. Some see changes, others are still waiting.

Our witnesses were at the March at varying stages in their lives. The youngest interviewed was thirteen years old, while the most seasoned was a revered newspaper reporter who had met and interviewed nearly all the major players involved. Without exception, they remember the "I Have a Dream" speech as the highlight of the day. There are other special memories as well: people wading in the Reflecting Pool, Mahalia Jackson whispering to Dr. King, the ebullience of riding on a freedom train.

Having grown up in the shadow of the Civil Rights Movement, I want my generation to hear the memories of the struggle. I sense a disconnect between my generation and that of the Civil Rights Movement. To some of us, forty years seems like an eternity ago. It is impossible for many to imagine living in American apartheid: giving up seats to a white person on a bus, drinking from a blacks-only water fountain, not being allowed to order a sandwich in a diner. We listened to our parents' records: Nina Simone, Aretha Franklin, and James Brown. We wanted to grow up and go to "Funky Nassau." We heard our parents singing "R-E-S-P-E-C-T, find out what it means to me…" and "Say, it loud, I'm black and I'm proud." By the time we were teenagers, it was no longer about the first black to do something, but the second and the third. So many of us don't think in color. As children of the movement, we now come in all colors—more than Baskin-Robbins. We belong to the world.

And the Civil Rights Movement made it all happen. We forget that forty years isn't that long ago, especially when we consider that today voting rights are under attack, homelessness is a major problem, and there is a backlash against affirmative action in education and employment.

Yes, the times, they are a 'changin'.

But when I did the research for *Like a Mighty Stream*, I was forced to do some soul-searching and some reconsidering. And to make some apologies to the generation before me. Today, we can be arrogant. But I learned that the sword cuts both ways. We must respect the past, especially the immediate past because it is so near that we can touch it.

When the esteemed journalist Evelyn Cunningham told me that every time she hears "We Shall Overcome" she wants to cry, her words made me want to cry.

For as long as I can remember, February was Black History Month, meaning that I would have to sing "We Shall Overcome" almost every day of that month. For years, as I joined in singing the song from elementary school to college, and at various banquets and memorial services as an adult, I swayed back and forth, joining hands with family, friends, classmates, neighbors and strangers. And I must confess that I didn't understand the true magnitude, the true meaning of the song until I began writing this book.

It is not a song for cynics. There is deep meaning in those words. In some ways the song is not always for the living, it is to honor those who did not overcome enslavement, degradation, and violence. It is for those who did not overcome the tyranny of Reconstruction and being denied an education, employment, fair housing, and the vote. It is for those who did not overcome feeling inferior, who never knew the greatness of their people. It is for those who did not overcome lynchings, skinnings, and bombings. And it is for those who did not overcome their own insecurity and allowed hatred and greed to overrule a sense of compassion and fairness.

On April 14, 2002, I went to Riverside Church in New York City—where, in 1963, 80,000 sandwiches had been assembled and shipped to the March on Washington—for a celebration of the Manhattan Country School's thirty-fifth anniversary. As I took my seat, I looked at the program. I passed over the theme, "Today's Children Salute the Children of the Movement," and went immediately to the end of the program, Item 19: All sing… "We Shall Overcome."

I looked up onstage at today's children—black, white, Asian, Latino, East Indian. Some wore dreadlocks and dungarees; others were more formal. And they opened their mouths and led an audience of adults into "Woke Up This Morning with My Mind Set on Freedom." I looked around the audience at proud graduates of

Manhattan Country School and their equally proud parents, who sang the song with wide smiles.

I, too, smiled.

And then my smile turned to tears as a succession of speakers— Ruby Bridges, Carolyn Goodman, Bob Zellner, Harry Belafonte, and John Lewis—accepted awards from young people, many half my age, who recounted how each recipient inspired them.

And no matter how many times one thinks that one has heard the story of a first grader sitting in a Louisiana classroom alone because parents refused to allow their children to attend class with her; or of a mother's anguish in hearing her son's voice for the last time before he is murdered—it is worth hearing again, to remind oneself how precious freedom is.

When it was time to sing "We Shall Overcome," I was already on my feet. I swayed back and forth, my eyes occasionally closed. I was amazed at how people who had been singing this song all their lives sang it as if they'd never sung it before—and how the youngsters sang it as if the song had just been written today.

I can only imagine the energy that filled the nation's capital on August 28, 1963, when more than 250,000 people joined in and sang those words.

Just the act of remembering is a tribute to the day and its purpose.

It is my hope that this book will bring back memories of August 28, 1963, and create new ones as well.

Freedom riders arriving in Washington, D.C.

CHAPTER 1

AUGUST 27, 1963:
ON OUR WAY
TO FREEDOMLAND

*A group from the Brooklyn, New York chapter of CORE, including
March committee member Anna Arnold Hedgeman, decided to make
the 237-mile trip on foot. They started out from New York on August
15 carrying signs that read "We March from New York City for
Freedom." Jay Hardon, 82, rode his bicycle from Dayton, Ohio.
Ledger Smith decided to roller-skate the 750 miles from Chicago,
wearing a bright red sash that read Freedom.*
—James Haskins

For thousands of Americans, August 27, 1963 was no ordinary
Tuesday. They were headed to Washington, D.C., where in less than
twenty-four hours they would become a part of one of the greatest
demonstrations the world had ever witnessed.

Community activists, who had raised funds selling buttons and
desserts, made numerous phone calls, and attended endless meetings
and rallies, would stand up and be counted. Lifelong members of
organizations like the National Association for the Advancement of
Colored People (NAACP), the National Urban League, the
Housewives League, Jack and Jill, and the National Council of Negro
Women would beam as they proudly carried picket signs. They would
lift their voices to the sky and sing freedom songs alongside other
groups: fraternities and sororities; the Elks and the Order of the
Eastern Star, members of the Student Nonviolent Coordinating
Committee (SNCC) and the Southern Christian Leadership
Conference (SCLC). They would share anecdotes with folks who had

established their own groups. Some members of this new breed had never attended a protest meeting in their lives; never sold a button, brought a cake, nor given much thought to joining professional organizations or other groups. Protestants, Catholics, Jews, and atheists would break bread as they shared sandwiches. These images (and more) would leave an indelible impression on high school and college students—bright-eyed, open-minded, just discovering the world, and deciding that it could do with some changes. They would hear no objections from elder folk—some just a generation or two removed from enslavement. Some were poor, scraping together their last $8 for a round-trip bus ticket to Washington, D.C. On Tuesday, they'd gone to bed early, knowing they'd have to beat the rising sun so that they could catch their bus. This was not a worry for some privileged captains of industry and their wives—they would arrive by plane. But they would arrive.

Like troops going into battle, not one of them could guarantee the outcome. They could not be certain that they would return home unharmed, uninjured, or even alive. They could not be certain if they would have their jobs. They didn't know if their neighbors would look at them in the same way tomorrow as they had the day before. They were traveling against the objections of parents, teachers, lovers, and dear friends.

But they *would* travel. They would board buses, planes, and trains because they were determined not to do the alternative: stay home, remain uncounted.

They wanted to do something.

This was a time like no other.

They had seen enough on television — blistering water hoses and barking dogs unleashed on tender-bodied children in Birmingham. They had read enough in newspapers—bombings, boycotts, and brutality.

They had seen enough with their own eyes. They had been devastated when they witnessed a black man and his family being denied hamburgers at a restaurant and told: "We don't serve niggers here." And they hadn't said anything—neither to the family nor the worker. They were sickened by this exchange, but yet they ate their meal, paid for it, even tipped the waitress. Maybe they didn't like trouble. They weren't confrontational.

But they were Americans.

And the images on television didn't disappear when Walter Cronkite signed off on the evening news. The sight of grieving mothers and weeping children awakened them from an uneasy sleep. They realized that this country was deeply divided along racial lines. And some members from each side of the dividing line wanted to do something about bridging this gulf, fixing the firmament—making things right.

People on both sides of the dividing line were tired— tired of being silent, biting their lips, holding their tongues. They were tired of shaking their heads at news bulletins, holding their hands to their mouths, wiping a tear at night, while the world slept. And on this day, as they listened to reports of riots and rebellions, they were ready to head to the *spectacle*.

They cast their fears aside.

They were on their way to Freedomland.

On August 27, 1963, Culie Vick Kilimanjaro, who under any other circumstances was considered unflappable by her colleagues at Dudley High School in Greensboro, N.C., was flustered. This dainty woman with delicate features—who had once been told by Martin Luther King, Jr., that she "favored" his wife, Coretta—couldn't find a babysitter for her three small children, John Marshall, Jr., Sybil and Heidi. The next day, she was planning to attend the March on Washington with her husband, John Marshall Kilimanjaro—if she could find a sitter.

She very much wanted to go, even though she knew only a few details about the March; namely, that it would be in Washington,

D.C., and that the speakers would include Roy Wilkins of the NAACP, Martin Luther King of SCLC, and Whitney Young of the Urban League. She knew that she and her husband would board buses sponsored by local Shiloh Baptist Church and their branch of the NAACP. She had been too busy to buy any buttons or make any placards. She participated in her community's civic organizations, but not as an activist. Like many who would join her, Culie Vick had few expectations.

Sidetracked by her babysitting dilemma, she didn't have a chance to keep up with the late-breaking news on the March on Washington. So she had no idea that at the same time that March organizers were holding a press conference to kick off what they hoped would be one of the most memorable days in American history, they were pleading with Malcolm X not to hold his own press conference lambasting the event. Malcolm X had been highly critical of the March, calling it "The Farce on Washington." The clever Muslim leader, who had been anchored in The Statler-Hilton Hotel, held court with the press, but in the end, held off on the press conference. But he would be a presence at the March.

Culie knew that there would be armed forces, but she wasn't aware that the District of Columbia's police chief, Robert V. Murray, had "assembled a force of 5,900 men—including 350 club-carrying firemen, 1,700 National Guardsmen and 300 newly sworn in police reserves. At nearby bases, 4,000 soldiers and marines were ready to cross the Potomac in helicopters if they were needed for riot duty."

She felt that the March would have opposition. Culie, unlike many who had grave concerns about the Ku Klux Klan and the American Nazi Party (led by George Lincoln Rockwell), felt a certain sense of safety in numbers. She hoped that the day would have a "strong showing" from lovers of freedom.

Still, she hadn't heard the rumors about potential riots, or the talk that the March would erupt into a morass of chaos in Washington, D.C.

She didn't know that District of Columbia commissioners were so concerned that an unfortunate incident would occur that they had declared a public emergency and decided to ban the sale of alcoholic beverages in all stores until the civil rights demonstration had ended.

She'd never felt compelled to march on Washington, but during the long, hot summer of 1963, something happened to her. Watching Birmingham schoolchildren being attacked by dogs and sprayed with skin-tearing water hoses alarmed her. Those children could have been students at her high school. They could have been her children. Nowhere did she feel safe or free. In her own town, two years before, four students at North Carolina Agricultural and Technical College gained international attention by staging a sit-in at Woolworth's, to incite social change. Yet, little had changed There was still a severe limit on how much money she could borrow from the bank even though she had great credit. These thoughts and others raced through her mind as she sought a neighbor to take care of her children. Whenever anyone asked her why she was going, she responded that she "couldn't think of any reason not to go." She was engulfed with a sense of uncertainty and surprise and the sense that with her mere presence she might be part of the push to end discrimination in jobs, housing, schools, and other fields in America.

On August 27, 1963, as Culie Vick worked the phone to find a babysitter and rushed to fix a lunch of fried chicken and sandwiches for herself and her husband, technicians laid miles of telephone, radio and television lines across the grass near the Washington Monument and Lincoln Memorial. The National Parks Service set up hundreds of folding chairs near the memorial.

At the same time, the Washington office of the March on Washington set up their headquarters on the monument grounds, not far from where some early marchers prepared to sleep. According to the *Richmond Afro American*, "75 volunteers painted signs and print-ed names and slogans. They were joined by hostesses, many of them urbanites coming in to sell the 'We Shall Overcome' brochures, and more than 200 ushers from the Interdenominational Church Ushers

Union—women in white uniforms and men in somber suits—who sold *Marching for Freedom* buttons."

Earlier that morning, more than three hundred volunteers formed a line at the renowned Riverside Church in New York City, and assembled more than 80,000 cheese sandwiches, packing each bag with a sandwich, marble cake, and an apple. A refrigerated truck would head for Washington the next day, at four in the morning.

According to James Haskins, author of *The March on Washington,* "three buses pulled away from Milwaukee, Wisconsin. Four busloads left St. Louis. Six buses left Birmingham, Alabama. Later in the day two trains left Chicago; others departed from Pittsburgh and Detroit. Yet another departed from Jacksonville, Florida, to make stops in Waycross and Savannah, Georgia, and in Richmond, Virginia. On the West Coast, a chartered plane carrying thirty celebrities—including Charlton Heston and Marlon Brando—took off from Lockheed Airport."

They would be joined by marchers from every region of the country, who wanted to make it known to elected officials that there was a dire need for a sweeping civil rights bill, to end the apartheid that existed in the United States.

By evening, Culie Vick located her babysitter. She prepared to go to bed early since she didn't want to be late for her bus. And as she slept, Dr. Martin Luther King, Jr. was wide-awake, working on the speech that he would deliver in a few hours. The half-moon provided dramatic backlighting for King to peer out of his window and see Washington's flawless geometric monuments—a perfectly shaped circle, rectangle, and obelisk. The city was empty, now. But soon, it would be filled with people. A century and 240 days after the signing of the Emancipation Proclamation, the nation was due for a progress report.

King would be among a group of powerful speakers who would issue that national report card before more than 250,000 witnesses, including Culie Vick Kilimanjaro.

CULIE VICK KILIMANJARO REMEMBERS

*"We were young, vibrant, energetic; striving to accomplish
something and help improve the community."*

My husband and I were members of the NAACP and we thought that we needed to do something about the race situation. From week to week, we didn't know what was going to happen. People were being killed because they were trying to do what was right. We couldn't stop at a hotel until we got to certain points. You couldn't even buy food in a sandwich shop. I was a librarian, but it didn't mean anything to some white people because I had no control over their behavior, which was protected by law. Most of what I discovered about the movement, I learned through the newspapers, and friends and colleagues talking. We didn't attend church. We're Jewish, and went to Temple. Some people are curious about why I converted to Judaism. I did it in the 1950s when I was a student at North Carolina College, which is now known as North Carolina Central. I believed that God was one. My husband felt the same.

All of the details from the March we got through word of mouth. I told my husband that I would like to go to the March. The NAACP and the churches were sponsoring three buses. You had to pay your own way, but that was fine with us. I've never seen so many people in one place before in my life. We were able to sit down by the Reflecting Pool. It was hot but we were dressed for the occasion. It was great seeing Marian Anderson. When Dr. King spoke, it was like The Lord had spoken. He was really fantastic. I could've listened to him speak all day. People were on tree limbs, just enraptured by his words. After he finished speaking, we felt rejuvenated. We felt like we were going to accomplish something. On the bus

27

ride home, we were kind of tired…

When Kennedy was killed it had an effect on our whole household. He was like a family member almost, because he was somebody who was trying to do something about this segregated situation.

Now, we can go to any restaurants we choose. There are no more segregated restrooms. We can do anything that anyone else could, if you have the money. Back then, there were certain things that you couldn't buy, like a house in certain neighborhoods. Banks had a limit on the money that they would loan to black folks. Knowing that there are a variety of fields in the area of education that people can go into that in those days they couldn't, like being an administrator, is a tremendous change. Just breaking through in law, engineering, banking was a major accomplishment. There were a few then, now they're many. We were young, vibrant, energetic; striving to accomplish something and help improve the community. I think that's why we started the *Carolina Peacemaker* in 1967. We've been telling the story of the black community in Greensboro for over 35 years. I'm still trying to make the community a better place.

Freedom in 1963: Mission Possible.

CHAPTER 2
1863: FREE, BUT NOT FREE

What we now want is a country—a free country not saddened by the footprints of a single slave and nowhere cursed by the presence of a slaveholder. We want a country which shall not brand the Declaration of Independence as a lie.
—Frederick Douglass

Looking back, it is difficult to imagine that for most black Americans in 1963—a century after President Abraham Lincoln signed the Emancipation Proclamation—life and liberty were incompatible and the pursuit of happiness was restricted.

Negroes could not vote in most of the Delta, and there was mass voter intimidation among Negroes in other sections of the country. Through redlining and restricted covenants (which forbade the selling of houses to blacks) there was rampant housing discrimination. In the segregated South, there were separate restrooms and restaurant entrances for Negroes, and separate water fountains. Negroes could not sit with whites at concerts, the theatre or the movies. Some diners refused to serve Negroes. Negroes could not swim in some public pools. Negroes did not serve on juries. Employment discrimination was not only widespread, but also understood and accepted. Although Negroes were tax-paying citizens, they were underrepresented in local, city, state, and federal jobs.

Why did thousands of Americans travel to the nation's capital on August 28, 1963? It was an effort to end these ugly remnants of slavery through an unprecedented civil rights bill that would make discrimination in this nation illegal.

Moving forward, the March on Washington was a compelling story of a people who had moved from enslavement to freedom. It was, in part, an acknowledgment that the story of African-Americans was one of incredible hope, endurance, and patience. The March was a unique opportunity to rewrite the official story; to restore a group of people to the nation's official text from outside its wide margins. The official story—passed along in civics classes and nightly news reports—had been overdue for major editing and revision. In a country that prided itself on its civility, members of this race were treated with hostility. In a nation that was an undisputed superpower, 19 million people were considered, by some, to be inferior. In a country where freedom of speech was sacred, they were without a voice.

If the 250,000 people in attendance at the March on Washington did not have an opportunity to address the nation individually, they did so with their collective presence. The descendants of the enslaved, the offspring of their owners, abolitionists, Confederate and Union soldiers, the children of immigrants, and Native Americans spoke out with their applause, chants, and cheers. Their presence spoke during moments of silence, and when they cried, laughed, and sang freedom songs. They made a memorable impression—these protestors of every color, every generation—on television audiences around the world. Simply, quietly, powerfully, they said it was time for a change. Time to make the story right. Time to honor the principles on which this country had been founded.

* * *

As with all great stories, the tale of how thousands of Americans in 1963 convened around the Lincoln Memorial has a back story. While the March was planned over a period of less than eight weeks, its roots go back much further.

The issue of equality for enslaved Africans in America—from 1617 to 1863—by presidents, politicians, the churches, and Supreme Court justices, was clumsily handled. The result? An awkward coexistence between those with freedom and those without it. Children were born into a system where they would never know freedom, and often not even their natural families. Bartered and sold like cattle, families seldom remained intact. American slavery was a cruel institution, wherein imported Africans were subjected to servitude to men who owned them.

This practice began gradually in the mid-17th century. The earliest Americans of African descent arrived in Virginia in 1617, not as slaves but as indentured servants. For at least forty years, they lived alongside the early settlers and fashioned a semblance of domestic bliss. Their marriages were legal, they served on juries, some even owned land. Although they tried to adapt to become New Americans, there was one obstacle that they could not possibly overcome: they were of African descent. According to Jacqueline Jones in *American Work*, Europeans could "adopt the English language, worship in Anglican churches, and profess loyalty to the British monarch" with ease, but this was not a possibility for the "colored" in America.

They were different—almost too noticeable.

By 1657, early American settlers became involved with the lucrative slave trade. Enslaved men and women cleared forests, built mansions, and worked feverishly at taming an obstinate earth that would come to produce bountiful crops of cotton, sugar, corn, and tobacco throughout the Mid-Atlantic states. They were forbidden to read and write. Their travel was monitored. If they were found guilty of plotting to escape, they were hanged.

When America revolted against British tyranny, thousands of blacks joined the American troops, hoping that their freedom would be granted. But once the colonies wrested themselves from underneath British rule and asserted their independence, there seemed to be no pressing need to extend freedom to all. Many of the founding fathers—signers of the Declaration of Independence—owned slaves.

Although there are black newspapers, various journals, diaries, and letters from this period, it is difficult to comprehend what it was like to have been born into enslavement. Newspaper reports during slavery were filled with stories of kidnappers returning children to plantations, slaves subjected to beatings with cow-skins and cattle prods, and public whippings. If they could not go home to their native land, why could they not build a home in the land that was chosen for them? If they were denied freedom, why couldn't the politicians and lawyers wipe the slate clean for their children? By the beginning of the nineteenth century, the enslaved population in the expanding America became a nameless, faceless "problem" for some, and a "cause" for others.

By mid-century, slavery had divided the nation between those who benefited from it economically and those who thought it was a moral outrage. Somewhere in the middle was President Abraham Lincoln, who had stated: "If I could save the Union without freeing any slave I would do it, and if I could save it by freeing all the slaves I would do it, and if I could save it by freeing some and leaving others alone, I would also do that. What I do about slavery, and the colored race, I do because I believe it helps to save the Union." His signature on the Emancipation Proclamation in 1863 is viewed by many as the first step towards ensuring freedom for black Americans.

The Proclamation is widely regarded as the first national order to have had a positive impact on the lives of black Americans. Lincoln's bold move to end slavery certainly put the machinery in motion for freedom.

Whether or not Lincoln made the choice to sign the Proclamation to penalize the Confederacy for its secession, or because he was a shrewd politician, he had taken a stand that no other President had taken since the founding of the country.

Slavery officially ended in 1865, with the enactment of the Thirteenth Amendment. According to David W. Blight in *Race and Reunion: The Civil War in American Memory,* "by the time the War ended, 620,000 soldiers had died, 60 percent of them Union and 40 percent of them Confederate. American deaths in all other wars combined through the Korean conflict totaled 606,000. In the North, 6 percent of white males aged 13-43 had died in the war; in the South, 18 percent were dead. Of the 180,000 African Americans who served in the Union army and navy, 20 percent perished. Diseases such as typhoid, dysentery, and pneumonia claimed more than twice as many as did battle."

The country was shattered.

As Blight notes, "America was still not old; its ruins were not those made hoary by years and beautiful by decay. But it was a country that had torn itself asunder—physically, politically, and spiritually. Some of its cities lay in rubble, large stretches of the Southern countryside were depopulated and defoliated, and thousands of people were refugees from any sense of home."

Among the homeless and hungry were thousands of former slaves granted freedom, but not fully emancipated.

As historian John Hope Franklin has observed, "a casual reading of the Emancipation Proclamation made clear that it did not set the slaves free. It was also clear that neither the Reconstruction amendments nor the legislation and Executive Orders of subsequent years had propelled African Americans much closer to real freedom and true equality. The physical violence, the wholesale disfranchisement, and the widespread degradation of blacks in every conceivable form merely demonstrated the resourcefulness and creativity of those white Americans who were determined to deny basic constitutional rights to their black brothers."

And therein lies one of the cruel legacies of slavery: to be free, but not truly free in a country that cherishes freedom "for all." Those "not truly free" were dealt yet another crushing blow in 1883 when the Supreme Court overturned the Civil Rights Act of 1875, which guaranteed some freedoms. From that moment on, in many parts of the South, "blacks were banned from white hotels, barber shops, restaurants, and theaters," asserts Franklin in *From Slavery to Freedom*.

After nearly two centuries of being considered "property" rather than free men and women, generations of newly freed blacks entered a world where their labor was seen as competition and their presence viewed with contempt. Worse yet, they could not be sure what terror the Ku Klux Klan and other hostile groups would inflict upon them. Although they tried to build and sustain families and communities, acquire an education and learn a skill or trade, their freedoms were still not guaranteed. Some ventured out West, where they developed their own schools, businesses, and churches. Others remained in converted plantations, working as sharecroppers. Some built farms. More than a few went off to college to become doctors, teachers, attorneys, and nurses. They attended church. They supported one another through mutual aid societies and civic clubs. They created public schools for their children.

Although their faith and patience were tested, they soldiered on, waiting for that critical moment when things would change. By 1941, their expectations began to rise. After all, there was a war on. Wouldn't every available hand be needed for the war effort? Their ancestors had served in the Revolutionary War, the Civil War, and World War I with the hope that they could gain freedom in full.

This time, they would rally once again to protect America's freedom, and finally, they were certain, claim it for themselves.

BOB ZELLNER REMEMBERS

*"My fondest memory was not of the ' I Have a Dream' speech,
though that was memorable, but the image of the SNCC,
CORE, SCLC, and NAACP kids, mostly SNCC, joining hands
in a huge circle just below the speakers' stand, and singing
our hearts to the heights."*

I heard about the March during the planning stage, as a field secretary of SNCC. I was working in the summer of '63 in bloody Danville, Virginia. I decided to attend because I thought it would be a good way to sum up all the suffering and brave work SNCC and the other organizations and individuals had been doing since the pace of civil rights agitation picked up following the February 1, 1960, lunch counter sit-ins in Greensboro, North Carolina.

I traveled with my new bride, Dorothy Miller Zellner. We were married in Atlanta on August 9, a day or so after I got out of jail in Danville. For our honeymoon, we drove to Mobile, Alabama to visit my family and then to California to see movement friends, and then to Corning, New York for a speaking engagement, and then to New York City to visit Dottie's folks, and then to D.C. for the March on Washington, and then to Atlanta to pick up our few personal belongings, and then to Boston where Dottie would run the New England SNCC office on Harvard campus and I would begin a two-year study of sociology at Brandeis University.

My expectations were that the March would be a militant challenge to a foot-dragging government—an angry, yet jubilant wake-up alarm to the nation that black America and its allies were demanding jobs, justice, and freedom from a backward, vicious South and a genteel racist North that continued to allow the Civil War to remain unfinished.

My fondest memory was not of the "I Have a Dream" speech, though that was memorable, but the image of the SNCC, CORE, SCLC, and NAACP kids, mostly SNCC, joining hands in a huge circle just below the speakers' stand, and singing our hearts to the heights. The "event" itself had been controlled with a heavy hand and what singing there was, Mahalia Jackson, the freedom singers, etc. was doled out sparingly so as not to incite the "mob." Breaking the rules by singing was our feeble attempt to protest the forced changing of our Chairman John Lewis's speech because it was too fiery and militant. That was yet another playing out of the differences between the young people in SNCC and Martin Luther King, "de lawd," as we sometimes irreverently referred to him, although we loved him.

It surprised me that some of the moderates demanded a change in John's speech and that the leadership went along with it. Another surprise was when Ms. Jackson leaned over and said to King, "tell them about the dream, Martin." He did and it saved the speech and the day and the rest is history, somewhat sanitized.

The impact the March had on me was that it provided dramatic proof that the sometimes quiet and always dangerous work we did in the Deep South had had a profound national impact. The spectacle of a quarter of a million supporters and activists gave me an assurance that the work I was in the process of dedicating my life to was worth doing.

It is hard to enumerate the changes the last forty years have witnessed. Formal and de jure segregation is dead for the moment. White supremacy and racism has learned to be more effective and less visible. White privilege can be maintained without the overt trappings of apartheid. Class can replace race as the great divide and "respectable" people are free to advocate and enable massive upward distribution of wealth without being seen as sexist, racist, or otherwise labeled.

The forces that constituted the target of the March those forty years ago are still in power and Martin Luther King, Jr. is now an emasculated saint of sweetness and light and "non-violence." Those who have elevated him and now sing his praises, did not sing his praises when he was preparing a radical poor people's march on Washington, and opposing the war in Vietnam. It goes without saying that our non-elected President and his family retainers have not adopted nonviolence as their weapon of choice in Afghanistan but rather the New World Order of continuous war, where the terrorists replace the worn out old Red Bear.

A gentle army marches to the Lincoln Memorial.

CHAPTER 3

1941: 10,000 NEGROES ON TO WASHINGTON

If organizations really want the President to issue an executive order to abolish discrimination in all government departments ... they will be willing to put aside every other consideration and use their resources to make the march on Washington effective. How much are they willing to sacrifice to show the country that colored people mean business?
—A. Philip Randolph

The original March on Washington, scheduled for July 1, 1941, was a precursor to 1963's massive gathering.

As the country prepared to wage battles in World War II, between fifty to one hundred thousand Negroes—Pullman porters, doctors, preachers, lawyers, businessmen, nurses, teachers, men, women, and children planned to walk down Pennsylvania Avenue carrying banners to protest discrimination in defense industry employment. There would be songs: "John Brown's Body Lies a'Mouldering in the Grave," "Before I'll Be a Slave, I'll Be Buried in My Grave," and "Go Home to My Father and Be Saved." There would be a procession—a mighty army that would move through the city's main thoroughfares to the Lincoln Memorial. And there would be this memory: President Roosevelt looking out at a sea of black, brown, and beige faces—the people who had delivered him into the White House. He would close his eyes in disbelief, and then open them once more to see standing before him A. Philip Randolph, the legendary leader of the Brotherhood of Sleeping Car Porters, and the leader of this movement. And the eloquent Mr. Randolph would tell the President that discrimination was unlawful. The war effort needed all hands on deck—including black hands. And Mr. Roosevelt would see that the people were behind their leader. The President would clear his throat, and address the crowd, and tell them that he understands their plight. And then he would tell them what they waited to hear: "Yes, discrimination is unlawful, so today, I am issuing an executive order banning discrimination within the defense industry."

And the crowd would burst into applause.

Roosevelt did issue Executive Order 8802 (which banned discrimination in defense industry practices), but the hoped-for exchange between Roosevelt and Randolph, before thousands of marchers, did not happen.

Yet, the 1941 March on Washington almost happened. And the planning sowed the seeds for what *would* happen in 1963. Randolph had assembled a powerful, nearly unbreakable coalition of civic leaders, clergy, and working class black Americans in 1941. Despite the passage of two decades, many of them would come together again on Wednesday, August 28, 1963. This time they would march on Washington.

* * *

By 1941, nearly half a million Negroes had migrated to the Midwest, West and Northeast, seeking better economic opportunities—although many Negroes still remained in the South. Those who moved though the burgeoning defense industry, although still recovering from the Depression, might put an end to unemployment, hunger, and unspeakable living conditions in Northern or Midwestern slums, Southern shanties and shotgun houses. Defense plants began to sprout like ragweed throughout the country. Readers leafing through the classified sections of *The Chicago Defender, The Afro American, The Norfolk Journal and Guide* could find jobs as maids, dishwashers, janitors and drivers, but none in the booming defense industry. In fact, a defense plant in Akron, Ohio had been singled out for praise by the black press in 1941, solely because it hired a single Negro employee.

Black contractors, machinists and builders responded to this lockout with meetings, which led to letter-writing campaigns to the press and local politicians. The leading headline in the February 15, 1941 edition of the *Richmond Afro American* was "Defense Job Bias Probed." The story involved the Virginia-based Hampton Builders' Association, which sent Present Roosevelt a "580-word resolution denouncing discriminatory practices against colored workers on National Defense housing projects." Many civic groups began to forward similar telegrams and letters to civil rights leaders. They were concerned that private firms and labor unions, which benefited from lucrative federal contracts, had discriminatory clauses excluding skilled black workers in their agreements. A project in Fort Eustis, Virginia, for instance, was often cited in the Washington black newspapers because they'd hired "2,000 white carpenters, and not a single Negro" for work.

Soon, these incidents caught the attention of A. Philip Randolph, the influential president and founder of the Brotherhood of Sleeping Car Porters. He was outraged at this rejection of the Negro workforce. As the leader of the first organized labor union of Negro member with the AFL-CIO, he was not only a master negotiator, but also one of the most admired leaders in the black community. His effort on behalf of the Pullman Porters was profound.

Despite valiant attempts to form a union, black porters on Pullman trains weren't successful until 1925, when Randolph, a magazine editor and labor advocate, led them in a David versus Goliath battle with the Pullman Company, one of America's corporate giants. When the brotherhood threatened to strike and take 10,000 Pullman Porters to Washington, the brotherhood's wages were raised, and a powerful labor union was formed.

Overnight, Randolph became an American icon. Commonly addressed as "St. Philip" and called a "space age Moses" by the black press and community, Randolph spent half his life on railroads, traveling more than 100,000 miles, meeting and greeting black leaders, other porters, and families. Everyday folks were inspired by his grace, courage, and dignity. He was a shining example of the best of who we are as Americans.

While touring the country in 1941, Randolph listened to stories of men and women—with children to feed, clothe, and shelter—who were refused jobs at defense plants. Transplanted Mississippians who had moved to Chicago's slums, Carolinians who were trying to make their way in New Jersey, Philadelphia and New York; weary families in parts of Ohio, Indiana, and Michigan, who were passed over for white workers. Outraged, Randolph began to speak out against discrimination in defense industries to black civic and union meetings, but no one in "high-up" places was listening.

Randolph, who had founded the magazine *The Messenger* in 1918, relied on his close ties with editors of the black press to write a series of stinging editorials, which most of the more than 500 black newspapers were pleased to print. On March 15, 1941, he penned an article titled "March of 10,000 Workers on Capital Called Way to Get Jobs" that was published in the *Washington Afro American*:

Colored Americans have a stake in national defense. It is a big stake. It is a vital and important stake.

But are we getting our stake?

Nobody cares anything about us. We are being pushed around.

The stake involves jobs. It involves equal opportunity for integration in the armed forces of the nation.

And what do we get?

Polite promises; sometimes, insults.

How can this stake be protected?

Our answer is:

Let the masses speak.

We cannot stop discrimination in national defense with conferences of leaders and the intelligentsia alone. While conferences have merit, they won't get desired results by themselves.

Around this time, Randolph's path crossed with Bayard Rustin, whose idiosyncrasies perfectly balanced Randolph's straightlaced demeanor. Rustin's commitment to social justice was deep, real, and unwavering. Rustin became interested in civil rights in 1932 with the Scottsboro Case, when nine black men in Scottsboro, Alabama were sentenced to death after being accused of raping two white women. The case became an international cause célèbre and attracted the burgeoning Communist Party. An aesthete and intellectual, Rustin flirted with the Communist Party, and soon organized the Young Communist League at the City College of New York. By 1941, he and Randolph had become friends.

Through his Communist ties, Rustin understood the power of mass mobilization. He believed that it would take an action that garnered national attention to get the President's attention. He thought that Randolph should go farther than his editorials, since Roosevelt was still silent on the issue of defense industry discrimination of black workers.

Roosevelt's reticence was surprising to many Negroes, considering their support for him. Black voters had felt betrayed by President Herbert Hoover in 1930, after he nominated John J. Parker to fill a vacancy in the Supreme Court. (Parker had allegedly said "participation of the Negro in politics is a source of evil and danger to both races.") Black voters overwhelmingly supported Roosevelt when he became President in 1932.

Those same voters, reeling from the bloody legacy of Jim Crow—the terror of lynchings, skinnings, and the violent destruction of all-black towns in the South, Midwest, and West—viewed Roosevelt's election victory with optimism. Perhaps, they thought, things would get better. As the threat of war escalated, the shadow of the Depression was still hovering over the black community.

Randolph, disappointed by Roosevelt's lack of response to this pressing issue, wrote another editorial, this one calling for a March on Washington. Here, in part, is what it said: "When women marched in demonstration in England and in America, they won the ballot. When the World War veterans marched on Washington, they secured the bonus. Let no black man be afraid. We are simply fighting for our constitutional rights as American citizens. Let us not be beaten, bewildered and bitter. Away with cynicism and defeatism. We are not saboteurs. We are not Quislings. We hold no allegiance to any alien state. This is our own, our native land. Let us fight to make it truly free, democratic and just. On to Washington, 10,000 Black Americans!"

Less than six weeks after Randolph's first editorial, the Negro Committee to March on Washington for Equal Participation in National Defense was formed. Randolph and Rustin planned to galvanize the black community in a manner that would secure maximum visibility, the attention of the President, and the world.

In one of the group's first official announcements, Randolph demanded that Roosevelt "speak out forthrightly on the problem and tell the world what this administration will and can do on behalf of the underprivileged minority groups in the city."

Though concerned about the issue, Roosevelt was consumed with the tension in Europe. In addition, the President had to contend with a strong Southern voting bloc, who could stall his New Deal legislation. Now, he reasoned, was not the time to engage in a divisive national campaign when the country should be uniting against Nazism, Communism, and Fascism, he thought. And for a while, time was on his side. Although the Committee had formed, there appeared to be little if any Negro support for the March. Roosevelt thought that he could buy more time. He dispatched his wife, Eleanor, to deal with this "Negro problem."

Understanding that Negroes needed to turn up the heat, Randolph wasted no time. On April 12, 1941, the *Afro American* published one of Randolph's most scathing editorials. Its purpose was twofold: to call Roosevelt out on his hypocrisy, and to shore up Negro support for the March. The editorial bore the title, "Why F.D.R. Won't End Defense Jim Crow." Here's what Randolph wrote.

President Roosevelt can issue an executive order tomorrow to abolish discrimination in the Army, Navy, Air Corps, Marines and on all defense contracts awarded by the Federal Government on account of race or color and discriminations against colored people would promptly end.

There is no question about this. Nor is this procedure new. It has been employed before this defense emergency. It will be used again.

Why does not the President, who is unquestionably a great humanitarian, with definite and high ideals, issue such an order in the interest of national unity and national defense? The answer is clear.

President Roosevelt, though nominally believing in justice for the colored man, has not been positively and profoundly stirred and convinced that colored people are entitled to rights, economic, political and social, like all other American citizens and that like white citizens, are determined to fight for them:

He is perfectly willing for the colored people to be appointed with the status of half-men, if they are willing to accept it. He takes this attitude not because he thinks it is right, but in order to avoid trouble with the die-hard Southern, anti-colored politicians.

As the President of the United States, a statesman and a politician, he will grant no more to anybody, regardless of race or color, than he is compelled to grant. Therefore, the problem of the colored man is to develop the methods and employ the pressures, organized mass pressures that our social and national experience shows will secure the maximum results for the benefit of the colored man in the national defense program for our general rights as American citizens.

Hence, in order to effectively grapple with the situation, plans for an all out march of ten thousand colored citizens on Washington is in the making, and a call will be issued in the next few weeks to colored people everywhere to keep in their minds, night and day, the idea that all roads lead to Washington and there we shall go by every means possible and present our demands that the President issue an Executive Order to abolish discrimination in all departments of the government and on all government jobs for national defense.

Randolph's editorial resonated with blacks in every region of the country. A date for the March was set: July 1, 1941. After the editorial was published, interest in the March gathered momentum. Organizers anticipated that more than 100,000 marchers would make the pilgrimage to the Lincoln Memorial.

When the Lincoln Memorial was chosen as the site, the statue was only forty-one years old. Commissioned thirty-six years after Lincoln had been murdered by John Wilkes Booth, the marble and limestone building was completed in 1922.

But the Memorial had been notable for black Americans for another groundbreaking gathering in Washington. In 1939, contralto Marian Anderson sang to the largest integrated group in the nation's history, after the Daughters of the American Revolution had denied her the opportunity to sing at Constitutional Hall. Eleanor Roosevelt resigned from the DAR, and joined 60,000 black and white Americans to attend Anderson's recital.

Headquarters for the March were centered on 125th Street in Harlem, New York. Randolph set out on a month-long trip through Atlanta and Savannah, Georgia; Jacksonville and Tampa, Florida; and Richmond, Virginia. At every stop he hammered home the same mantra: "Negroes can no longer depend on outside agencies as the philanthropic foundation for solving our economic problems. The future of the Negro depends entirely upon this action, and one individual cannot act alone. This period calls for mass action, for in mass action, there is power."

Local committees were formed, with chairmen Thomas A. Webster in Kansas City, Miss E.M. White in Jacksonville, William Y. Pell in Atlanta, and Sidney R. Williams in Cleveland. Other committees were formed in Memphis, St. Louis, Trenton, and Baltimore. More than 50,000 buttons for the March were distributed throughout New York City. Saturdays in New York had been set aside as "Button Day"—young women sold buttons for 10 cents to help defray expenses. They held bake sales, dinners, and other fundraising events to pay for expenses to Washington. Randolph called on the Brotherhood of Sleeping Car Porters to visit churches and schools, shops and bars, to publicize the March.

After a successful tour through major cities to shore up support, the March on Washington Committee issued a statement on May 10, 1941, which read in part:

"In this period of power politics, nothing counts but pressure . . . through the tactics and strategy of broad, organized, aggressive mass action. We summon you to mass action that is orderly and lawful, but aggressive and militant, for justice, equality and freedom. We can build a mammoth machine of mass action with a terrific and tremendous driving and striking power that can shatter and crush the evil fortress of race prejudice and hate, if we will only resolve to do so and never stop until victory comes."

By May 24, 1941, with less than six weeks before the March, groups had been organized in Washington, D.C.; Richmond, Philadelphia, Trenton, Jersey City, Newark, Jacksonville, Atlanta, and Chicago, with several other cities developing committees. Churches, fraternal orders, women's clubs, labor organizations, non-partisan groups, civic clubs, youth groups, social service agencies and social clubs began to strengthen their delegations. Then, as in 1963, the mainstream media—including major metropolitan newspapers—paid little attention to the March. But the March was front-page news in black newspapers across the country, particularly the *New York Amsterdam News*, and *The Afro American*, a group of Washington, D.C. area newspapers.

President Roosevelt, intent on stopping the March, sent his wife Eleanor to persuade Randolph. Mrs. Roosevelt, immensely popular among blacks, told Randolph she knew that racial discrimination was not right. But she was convinced that the March was the incorrect method of protest. She said that her husband, the President, was sympathetic to the Negro cause, but feared that a melee would erupt in Washington, and people would get hurt. Randolph remained steadfast that the March would go on.

On June 13, less than two weeks before the March, Eleanor

Roosevelt, along with Aubrey Williams, the head of the National Youth Administration; Anna Rosenberg, regional director of New York City's Social Security Board; and New York City mayor Fiorello LaGuardia, met with Randolph and Walter White at City Hall. The meeting was a last-ditch effort to end the March. Again, Randolph insisted that the March would go on.

Now, black media began to rally around the March, some newspapers going as far as to suggest that all major civil rights organizations cancel their annual convention, and direct their members to Washington on July 1, 1941. Randolph argued vigorously for the March, saying "There will never be another opportunity such as this one. If these organizations really want the President to issue an executive order to abolish discrimination in all government departments, including the army, navy, air corps and national defense jobs, they will be willing to put aside every other consideration and use their resources to make the March on Washington effective. How much are they willing to sacrifice to show the country that colored people mean business?"

It began to seem certain that the March would take place. Delegations from many states, North and South, planned to go by train, car, and bus to Washington and join in the demonstration. At least 100,000 people (maybe more) were expected.

Realizing that the March would proceed, President Roosevelt summoned Randolph and White to the White House on June 18. It was a historic moment. The patrician Roosevelt and the refined Randolph, were both wily and witty, gifted orators and leaders. Roosevelt tried to bring levity to the situation by sharing benign anecdotes, but Randolph was there to take care of business. Taking cues from Randolph, Roosevelt decided to do just that.

On the eve of the August 28, 1963 March, Randolph recounted the story in *The New York Times* and *The Washington Post:*

"Now, Phil what do you want me to do?" asked the President.

"I want Negroes to be permitted to work in defense industries while other Negroes are fighting overseas."

"I'll call up the heads of the departments and get that done," the President said.

"But Mr. President, We want something concrete done. We want it done by executive order."

"I can't do that," the President said. *"I would be beset by other groups from time to time to issue orders. Now, Phil, I want you to call off this march.'*

"I can't do it unless you issue the order."

"How many people do you plan to bring?"

"One hundred thousand, Mr. President."

Soon after, President Roosevelt turned the impasse over to Cabinet officials to discuss a strategy for handling the March. Fiorello LaGuardia, who attended the discussions as Mayor of New York City, warned the others that Randolph would march unless an order was issued.

Weighing his options, Roosevelt did what he felt was the right thing for the nation.

"In the next day or two," Randolph recalled, "the order was issued and it had a profound effect. The President later told me he was proud to have the order issued in his administration."

On June 25, the President signed Executive Order 880, which "called upon both employers and labor unions to provide for the full and equitable participation of all workers in defense industries, without discrimination because of race, creed, color or national origin." Additionally, the Fair Employment Practices Commission was established to "investigate grievances, monitor compliance, and publicize its findings."

Randolph issued a statement that a march on the capital would not be in the best interests of colored people in the face of the

President's executive order banning racial discrimination.

Never in the history of the United States had a President issued an executive order that both condemned racial discrimination as a policy and aided black Americans economically.

"If The Emancipation Proclamation chipped away at physical enslavement, President Roosevelt's order was seen by many as the first step in curbing economic slavery. The 1941 action led to the creation of the Negro Committee to March on Washington for Equal Participation in National Defense, which would later re-name itself the March on Washington Movement and plan, among many public events, the August 28, 1963 March."

Reaction to the March's cancellation was mixed. Many Negroes were pleased by the executive order, and saw it as a sign of changing times. But others, like Roy Wilkins of the NAACP, were a bit more cautious. The same week that the March was called off, Wilkins wrote in his syndicated Watchtower column:

We ought not think this order means that Mr. Roosevelt woke up all indignant one morning and out of his sense of justice and fair play decided to issue an order on the Negro. Mr. Roosevelt is for all out aid to Britain, and perhaps for a 'defense' effort that will be useful to this country in war. His decree is strictly in the interest of defense production.

If he had been interested in racial discrimination, he could have found (and still can find) hundreds of chances to swat it right under his nose in the nation's capital. He could look in the Government departments, the Army and Navy, and a dozen other places and he could have acted long ago had he so desired. The most important of them, of course, is that this action was forced on the Administration by the March on Washington crusaders. Proving once more that we get more when we yell than when we plead.

Still, there was optimism in the air. As African Americans joined the war effort as Buffalo Soldiers and WACS, as they went to work in factories alongside Rosie the Riveter, and began to build better security for their families, there was a sense that things could get better. But a potential victory abroad did not always mean a future victory for civil rights. By the late 1950s, many leaders wondered aloud how life might have been different if 100,000 Negroes had marched on Washington.

Three of the key figures of the 1941 effort—Randolph, Rustin, and Wilkins—would unite for the planning of the August 28, 1963 March.

Rosa Parks in a moment of reflection at the March on Washington.

ED BRADLEY JR. REMEMBERS

". . . the March was bigger than anything that I'd ever experienced. There'd never been a demonstration like that in our lifetime. It was a feeling that we'd done something special; we were a part of something special."

I started hanging around WDAS radio station in Philadelphia. I was interested in radio broadcasting. There was a disc jockey there, Georgie Woods, who was very popular, and very involved in the Civil Rights Movement. George decided to charter buses for the March on Washinton, and paid for them out of his own pocket. He asked me to be one of the bus captains. As a captain, you were responsible for your bus, and everyone on it. You made sure that everyone got on, off, and back home. We had a caravan of about six or seven buses. All of the buses were full. The first sense that I had of the March was a lot of people walking down Constitution Avenue. You didn't have a sense of the magnitude of the people attending until you got to the Washington Monument. When you're in it, you're caught up in the moment, and it's hard to be contemplative. But I realized that the March was bigger than anything that I'd ever experienced. There'd never been a demonstration like that in our lifetime. It was a feeling that we'd done something special; we were a part of something special. Dr. King's speech was so powerful and captivating that it drowned everything else out. On the way home, I remember people being tired. But their spirits were still buoyed. Coming back, people threw rocks at our buses several points along the way back to Philadelphia.

At the time, I was in a strange position. I was majoring in elementary school education, and was about to become a school teacher. Eventually, I taught school. But I was also able to get on the radio at WDAS ... I knew in my heart that I was meant to be in radio broadcasting, but I didn't know how to get on the air.

If you look at every profession, I think that things have changed. I can remember when the first African American was hired as a Greyhound bus driver. I can remember when I saw the fist African American reporter on the news; now it's commonplace. You see the space program and see people as scientists and astronauts. You can look at *Black Enterprise* and see a number of successful businesses. We can look at Ken Chenault at American Express or Dick Parsons at AOL/Time Warner. These are major changes. Forty years ago, there were some white-owned companies that wouldn't sell products to black Americans, much less hire us.

Significant gains have been made in housing, education, voting, and employment, but today we have the right to vote, but we don't exercise it. That applies to all Americans. I think that voting is key to choosing your own future, and the people who will represent you.

Crowds gather around the Reflecting Pool. There is power in mass action.

CHAPTER 4
THE NEW FRONTIER

I am not satisfied with an America where the minimum wage
is only $1 an hour…22 million Americans live in slums…
Ralph Bunche must work with the United Nations because
Washington, D.C., is not fair to his children…Nor am I satisfied with
an America where not a single Negro federal judge has been
appointed since the Democrats put Judge Hastie on the bench more
than a decade ago. I do not intend to keep things as they are.
I am not going to stand still—I am going to move to the New Frontier.
There on the frontier is where I propose to take my stand—where no
one cares what color your skin is—where no one asks what church you
go to—where no one asks where your parents were born.
There is work for us all on that New Frontier.
—Senator John F. Kennedy,
on the presidential campaign trail in 1960

In 1960, black Americans looked cautiously to the future, and for the first time in a long while, that future held promise. John F. Kennedy's candidacy for President signaled the beginning of a new covenant between the leader of the free world and the black community. The previous decade had seen some advances for black Americans, particularly in the Northeast and Midwest, where black men and women began to find work in the booming manufacturing sector and in civil service after World War II. But their numbers were few. In 1963, "one and a half million Negroes were unemployed. Although Negroes made up 11 percent of the work force, they comprised 22 percent of the jobless. In 1963, 25 percent of the American people lived below the poverty line. In fact, the economic gap between whites and blacks was widening rather than narrowing, as it had immediately after World War II."

After the great migrations of the twentieth century, most black folks decided to settle in for the long haul in their newly adopted homes. They would have to forge ahead in unfamiliar surroundings. Change was in the air, but no one could predict how it would manifest itself.

It is often said that children will lead the way. And it was a child—10-year-old Linda Brown of Topeka, Kansas—who paved the way for monumental change in 1954.

Linda had to walk past the white elementary school minutes away in her own community—*and* maneuver through a train yard—to catch a bus to an all-black school miles away. Her father, Oliver Brown, sued the Topeka Board of Education to allow his daughter to attend the school nearby. The case wound up in the Supreme Court. On May 17, 1954, the justices ruled in *Oliver Brown et al V. the Board of Education of Topeka, Kansas* that segregation in public schools was illegal. This was a stunning victory for supporters of civil rights. There was, indeed, change in the air.

It was also apparent that many wanted to maintain the status quo. This was evident in many ways, including the brutal murder of four-teen-year-old Emmett Till. While visiting relatives in Money, Mississippi, the Chicago native—bright-eyed, confident, charming—whistled at a white woman, and was mauled by a gang of white men, who, after beating him to death, tied a gin-mill fan around his neck, and threw his body into the Tallahatchie River.

The white men's eventual acquittal by an all-white jury was a sharp blow to the sensibilities of black communities, and fair-minded people everywhere.

The same year that Till was murdered, no one watching the evening news could deny the courage and sincerity of boycotters in Montgomery, especially after seeing Rosa Parks, a forty-three-year old seamstress, arrested after refusing to give up her seat on a segregated bus.

Black folks saw the noble, gentle, and proper Parks being fingerprinted and arrested for ... *for what*? Not giving up her seat to a white person at the end of a workday? Parks was the sweet-faced woman in everyone's collective black memory. They felt they knew her. She was a dutiful daughter and devoted wife. She was civic-minded. She had impeccable southern manners. If this could happen to Parks, it could happen to any black person in the South. And if blacks in parts of the South were still living in the shadow of Jim Crow and its overt racism, those in the Northeast and Midwest were still trying to navigate through a maze of bureaucratic racism: redlining and widespread employment discrimination. For every white person who made Parks give up her seat, there was another deciding black folks' fate at work, the bank, and in Northern and Midwestern schools. The Parks incident struck a nerve as people recounted the incident in churches, factories, beauty parlors, and barbershops across the country. Miles away from Montgomery, black folks united around a common cause: civil rights.

In Montgomery, outraged citizens chose to boycott the public bus system until all citizens were afforded an equal right to a bus seat. For many, it meant walking several miles, twice a day, between their homes and jobs. Eye-opening stories about the boycotts ran in the *Chicago Defender, Pittsburgh Courier,* and *Norfolk Journal and Guide.* The term "country" could not apply to these willful black walkers, who represented every shade of black. The women were elegant and poised, scarves and pearls adorning their long necks; the men mighty and proud, in dungarees and two-piece suits. The Montgomery boycotters—young and old, farmer and professional—made a lasting impact on the psyche of black Americans.

On front porches in the South and stoops in the North, there was talk of missing children, violated daughters, wounded sons, dead husbands, and frightened wives. There was also talk that something must be done, and if blacks could not gain support from the government, then where could they turn? They would have to turn to themselves, rely on their own resources. Build coalitions. Venture out, on faith, into a new experience, that could be dangerous but could also lead to a better way.

There were signs of hope. Eisenhower's eleventh hour summoning of the National Guard into the Little Rock, Arkansas integration crisis in 1957 met with approval in the black community. Yet, there was still concern for the nine children once the troops left Central High. What horrible names had the children been called? Was it true that they had been spat upon? Were their parents threatened? Could they be killed?

And the images—not just the clean, well-scrubbed faces of the Little Rock Nine, but the puzzling scenes of Southern white mothers and fathers, in similar starched outfits, with piercing eyes and pursed mouths—were unsettling. These were not white folks in white sheets. They looked as if they walked off the set of *Leave it to Beaver* or *Ozzie and Harriet.*

How could the black community battle a group of people who said grace—with feeling—every evening, but during the day, carried banners proclaiming "Nigger, Go Home!" and "Don't You Wish You Were White?"

Every movement needs a face, a name, and a voice. And this nameless, faceless, voiceless movement soon found all (and more) in Dr. Martin Luther King Jr., a Baptist preacher based in Montgomery, Alabama, who combined sermons and speeches into a poetic clarion call.

King and a new breed of young black leaders kept violence against blacks and civil rights workers at the forefront of the nation's domestic agenda, as the country prepared to elect a new President in 1960. They made themselves difficult to ignore.

Yet, while civil rights had become the top issue for black voters, it hardly registered for non-blacks, consumed as they were with an economic slowdown that would last until 1963. Factory orders had begun to decline, and there was talk of massive layoffs. GI's who had taken long-term, low-interest loans to purchase model homes in the suburbs and brand new cars, did not find the economic slump welcome news.

The 1960 election was far more interesting than the previous battle between Eisenhower and Adlai Stevenson, in which, Carl Rowan noted, black voters felt "trapped between the devil and the witch."

In the early days of the election, Vice President Richard Nixon—jowly, jittery, and tightly wound—garnered support from black voters. *The Negro Digest* pointed out that he "had traveled to Africa and was photographed shaking the hands of tribal villagers and holding African babies." And Nixon had three black advisors—E. Frederic Morrow, Val Washington, and former baseball star Jackie Robinson—who guided him on civil rights issues.

Conversely, Kennedy had few Negroes as personal friends, and initially wasn't well versed on civil rights. Writing in *Ebony*, Simeon Booker pointed out that Kennedy was "no tub-thumping liberal; he was decidedly not Minnesota Senator Hubert Humphrey, or Illinois Senator Paul Douglas," staunch progressives.

When Kennedy named Texan Lyndon B. Johnson the vice presidential candidate, "Frank Reeves, who had been appointed by Kennedy to oversee race relations, had to advise Johnson to keep his wife from talking too much about her good friend, her Negro maid," Booker wrote.

Kennedy did have a slight edge with black voters. He appeared assured, athletic, and approachable. Booker believed that "unlike Presidents Roosevelt and Truman, Kennedy would be more accessible for meetings with Negroes—not arranged through a maid or valet—and that he would be more sympathetic to civil rights issues because the Democrats were relying heavily on their vote."

But early in the election, both Nixon and Kennedy played it safe on issues of race, developing moderate civil rights planks at their national conventions that would not alienate the Southern voting bloc.

Two months before the general election, many voters were still undecided.

In late October, Dr. King was lodged in a Georgia jail. Recounting the incident in a November 1961 article, "Did a Phone Call Elect Kennedy President?," *The Negro Digest* reminded readers of the significance of Kennedy's call to Coretta Scott King when "Nixon refused to call King or make a statement." This snub came on the heels of Nixon abandoning "speaking engagements in Negro sections of Northern cities; and his quietly playing down civil rights as a campaign theme."

Nixon, convinced that he would carry Southern states, said, "such an intervention would have damaged his election plan. As expected, there was a shift in sentiment—aided, perhaps, by the showering of millions of leaflets in black communities," pointing to the Democratic candidate's bold plank; and a candidate who "declared the president should use his executive authority to wipe out racial discrimination in every field of federal activity, and lead the fight for even stronger civil rights."

In a stroke of bravado, Kennedy called King's wife, Coretta, who had emerged as a beloved figure in the black community. King's wife remarked later that she still hadn't heard from Nixon. Overnight, "there was a re-evaluation of the candidate whose religion was his main stumbling block in penetrating the highly-Protestant vote bloc."

Kennedy began to gain momentum. In Philadelphia, "thousands of Negroes lined the streets and crowded a housing area to hear the young Senator. It was the first sign of 'acceptance' by Negroes in the campaign, but Kennedy had some difficulties: the mikes broke down."

By mid-week, black folks on the West Coast "jammed an auditorium to hear Kennedy, and aides knew them that they had finally struck gold," the *Negro Digest* reported.

Many black voters saw Kennedy's proposed New Frontier initiative as a means to ending their second-class status. In the article "What Negroes Can Expect from Kennedy," Simeon Booker detailed the New Englander's plans to focus on "education, medical care, health, increased wages, and employment. The proposal to offer scholarships to bright youngsters unable to afford higher education was seen as a godsend to hundreds of qualified black youth.

Rebuilding of cities, not only providing jobs, was seen as the first step in eliminating slums and making it possible for Negroes to enjoy clean, modern housing."

During the campaign, Kennedy quietly but firmly carried out his New Frontier approach to race relations. "When hotels in two cities refused to house Negro members, Kennedy ordered the three-plane caravan to return to Washington."

On Tuesday, November 8, 1960, John F. Kennedy was elected president of the United States, with one of the slimmest margins of victory in history.

"The slim margin of victory was due to the heavy vote of Negroes in strategic northern and southern states. Many black civic leaders made no secret that their constituents had delivered Kennedy into the White House, and at last, they would have a president who would deliver on his campaign promises of a unified America, in which all of its citizens were treated equally."

The election was also a wake-up call to white Southerners. After all, the black vote helped to deliver a president. They feared that this new Negro political power would change the way they lived their lives, forever.

Once in office, "the President took modest steps to implement some of the civil rights promises made during the campaign." But core Democrats were disappointed that Kennedy "refused to honor his pledge to end discrimination in federally assisted housing with a stroke of the pen because it was politically disadvantageous."

For a generation of young people who experienced the bus boycotts, *Brown v. Board of Education*, sit-ins and civil disobedience, the Freedom Rides and Freedom Trains, the activities of the Southern Christian Leadership Conference and the Southern Nonviolent Coordinating Committee, it was clearly time for a civil rights bill.

In February, Kennedy sent his first civil rights package to Congress, which spelled out plans to expand the role of the Civil Rights Commission, plus proposals for technical and economic assistance to school districts in the process of desegregation. While it was more thorough than any civil rights message thus far, civil rights leaders thought that it had been watered down and would not advance the cause.

The President and other leaders worked hard to ensure passage of the bill. Its fate would play a major role in both determining the President's reputation for leadership and setting the stage for the election of 1964. Kennedy held an unprecedented series of private meetings with civil rights activists, explaining the difficulties he faced in Congress, "You have to remember that I'm in this, too, right up to my neck."

In 1963, Birmingham, Alabama was considered the most segregated city in the country, "the last stop before Johannesburg, South Africa." At the beginning of the year, the SCLC had mounted an aggressive campaign to desegregate the City of Steel. While the black business community and black elite were reluctant to participate in these organized efforts, many black residents were prepared to break the stronghold of the city's white power structure, led by the notorious Bull Connor, Birmingham's police commissioner.

The Sixteenth Street Baptist Church in Birmingham became the movement's headquarters. There, leaders made speeches, and developed strategies for boycotts, sit-ins, freedom walks and rides as part of a campaign to focus attention on Birmingham. They wanted to put the nation's deficient civil rights policy on the national (and international) stage.

The determined Birmingham black community—young and old—marched, rallied, filling jails with black bodies as they were arrested for civil disobedience.

On Good Friday, April 12, 1963, King and his associate Ralph Abernathy were arrested. They were prepared. Connor had given them exactly what they wanted. They'd "donned stiff new jeans, covered their white collars with blue work shirts, and led fifty marchers to the police vans, escorted by a large crowd of supporters, reporters, and cameramen."

From his cell, King wrote his stirring "Letter From a Birmingham Jail," an impassioned plea for civil rights, and a blueprint for the movement's mission.

On Friday, May 3, 1963, the lead story on the evening news showed children—mainly high school students preparing to protest—being sprayed with fire department water hoses, and attacked by police department German shepherds. Newspapers around the world carried the story the next day.

People throughout the world looked to Kennedy for his reply. The smooth-tongued President struggled for the appropriate reaction. In *A Question of Character*, author Thomas C. Reeves asserts that Kennedy's top aides believed "that racial issues would take care of themselves as "they devoted their attention to other matters. [It] was a rational policy that might have worked a few years earlier. But Kennedy underestimated the passion for justice within the Civil Rights Movement—because [he] did not share it. [He] failed to realize that [his] eloquent campaign rhetoric about equality and democracy would not be taken seriously by people who had suffered long enough."

Kennedy and his brother Robert, who was the Attorney General, "became deeply involved in civil rights through events rather than planning, through necessity rather than philosophy, through emergency rather than deliberation," Reeves wrote.

On the same day, Governor George Wallace barred the door of the University of Alabama's administration building to Deputy Attorney General Katzenbach and two black students seeking to enroll under the provisions of a federal court order.

Kennedy's advisors warned him that he could upset the Southern voting bloc if he made too forceful a statement against segregation. Yet, on June 11, Kennedy felt compelled to respond to this offensive image of a public official keeping two students from an education. So in a fifteen-minute speech beginning at eight o'clock Eastern

Standard Time, he addressed the nation:

> *One hundred years of delay have passed since President Lincoln freed the slaves, yet their heirs, their grandsons are not fully free. They are not freed from the bonds of injustice; they are not yet freed from social and economic oppression. And this nation, for all its hopes and its boasts will not be fully free until all its citizens are free... We preach freedom around the world, and we mean it. And we cherish our freedom here at home ...*
>
> *But are we to say to the world—and much more importantly to each other—that this is the land of the free, that we have no class or caste system, no ghettoes, no master race, except with respect to Negroes?*
>
> *Now the time has come for this nation to fulfill its promise. The events in Birmingham and elsewhere have so increased the cries for equality that no city or state or legislative body can prudently choose to ignore them.*
>
> *The fires of frustration and discord are burning in every city, North and South ... We face, therefore, a moral crisis as a country and a people. It cannot be met by repressive police action. It cannot be left to increased demonstrations in the streets. It cannot be quieted by token moves or talk. It is time to act in the Congress, in your state and local legislative body, and, above all, in all of our daily lives ...*
>
> *Those who do nothing are inviting shame as well as violence. Those who act boldly are recognizing right as well as reality.*

Although the speech had been choppy and hastily pasted together, it had the sincerity of a Henry Fonda performance, and was just as effective.

The optimism the speech generated might have lasted for days if it were delivered on any other night. But on that very night—the first time an American president had ever spoken against segregation—Mississippi NAACP leader Medgar Evers was murdered outside his home in Jackson, Mississippi.

Kennedy decided to devise a civil rights bill that would call for "federal authority to guarantee blacks the right to be served in public places, to attend an integrated school, to receive federally financed training and education, and to look for a job without fear of discrimination."

The Southern Democratic bloc banded together to defeat any legislation, and began to increase their rhetoric, accusing civil rights leaders of being influenced by Communist agitators. Kennedy's Northern Democrats supported him, while Republicans decided to offer their own civil rights plan.

The New York Times predicted that the struggle for a civil rights bill on Capitol Hill would be long and often bitter. Vice Prsident Lyndon Johnson privately expressed pessimism about the success of any civil rights legislation. Several black leaders said they would ignore Kennedy's appeal for restraint during the congressional debates and continue demonstrations. To Kennedy's horror, there was talk of a "massive march" on the Senate and House galleries.

While Kennedy was obsessed with other trails on this new frontier—the space program, technology, public works—he knew that he had to continue on the uncharted and untested waters of a civil rights dilemma that showed no signs of going away.

As the seasons changed from spring to summer, Justice Department records showed 978 demonstrations in 109 cities over a four-month period.

Now, Congress appeared more amenable to devising civil rights legislation. But what kind? There had been too much bloodshed, too many lives lost to settle for a watered-down bill. For the bill to have meaning, the black community would have to send a powerful message to Washington. What this message would say was on the mind of A. Philip Randolph, who would prove that there was strength left in the mighty lion who had stared down Franklin D. Roosevelt.

BEVERLY ALSTON REMEMBERS

"It was a very noisy day. Everyone was singing and there were babies resting on their fathers' shoulders. Dr. King seemed to sum up everyone's feelings of the time with his speech. Everyone was friendly, sharing, caring. I remember people turning the Reflecting Pool into a swimming pool. I remember seeing thousands and thousands of feet. I was one of the lucky ones able to touch the water."

I first heard about the March on Washington when I participated in a leadership training program sponsored by HARYOU, a federally-funded, anti-poverty program, made available through legislation sponsored by New York Congressman Adam Clayton Powell, Jr. It ran under the aegis of noted psychologist Dr. Kenneth B. Clark, sociologist Cyril Tyson, and Rev. Eugene Calender, and it was the precursor to the community action programs that permeated the 60s and 70s. It substantiated the study by Dr. Clark entitled, "Youth in the Ghetto," which became the research document, in part, for funds for President Johnson's War on Poverty.

I was one of thirty-two youth participants, age 14-20, identified for my leadership potential to become a member of HARYOU. I was recommended by my eighth grade teacher, although I was a year below the age requirement. The powers that be decided that we should participate in the March on Washington since it was the goal of the program to expose the trainees to the Civil Rights Movement and the March was in support of civil rights legislation. Having been born and raised in Harlem, I had never experienced overt racism (or so it seemed up to that point). I had never participated in any form of demonstration before that time, although many of the other, older trainees had participated in demonstrations and sit-ins in their schools and throughout the South. I remembered thinking on that day that perhaps it was a last minute decision for the leadership trainees to attend because we seemed to be the only group from New York on a school bus, unlike the "adults" who had the comfort of riding in luxury buses.

My fondest memories of the day—which still seems the hottest day in history—was the amount of people in attendance. It was a very noisy day. Everyone was singing and laughing. There were babies resting on their fathers' shoulders. Dr. King seemed to sum up everyone's feelings of the time with his speech. Everyone was friendly, sharing, caring. I remember people turning the Reflecting Pool into a swimming pool. I remember seeing thousands and thousands of feet. I was one of the lucky ones able to touch the water.

The March brought the realization of the struggle to me, and it certainly contributed to the successful implementation of civil rights legislation at that time, and keeping its memory alive serves to continue the progression ... albeit not necessarily race-based.

Culturally, there has been tremendous progress over the past forty years. Black awareness and self-determination has soared. Politically, I just don't think that we've made enough progress.

Extra! Extra! Spreading the great news about the March on Washington.

CHAPTER 5

LADIES AND GENTLEMEN OF THE PRESS . . . THE MARCH IS ON!

On May 17, 1957, three years after the Brown v. Board of Education decision, more than 30,000 people congregated at the Lincoln Memorial for a Prayer Pilgrimage. The gathering was significant, bringing together black political and civil rights leaders, entertainers, clergy, and everyday citizens. The crowd listened to rousing speeches from New York Congressman Adam Clayton Powell and Roy Wilkins of the NAACP, a dynamic hymn from Mahalia Jackson, and a remarkable speech from a young pastor from Montgomery named Martin Luther King, Jr. Indeed, at the Prayer Pilgrimage, it is safe to say that in King, a new leader was born.

The Prayer Pilgrimage was momentous. It reunited A. Philip Randolph (who introduced King to the crowd) with Bayard Rustin. It would later provide a blueprint for the 1963 march. At its core, the Pilgrimage was about the passage of the Civil Rights Act of 1957.

The tens of thousands who assembled in Washington, D.C., to celebrate the third anniversary of *Brown v. Board of Education* served as a testament to Rustin's unparalleled relationship with a broad and diverse coalition of progressive leaders. The celebrities in the crowd—including actors Ruby Dee, Harry Belafonte, Sidney Poitier, and Sammy Davis, Jr.—were also proof of his uncanny ability to put on a "show."

After the abandoned 1941 march, Rustin kept busy. He had seen the power of nonviolent protest while in India. He traveled to Montgomery during the bus boycotts, and suggested that the boycotters "embrace opposition in the name of Gandhi, to dramatize that the real enemy was the system." While there, he recognized the leadership potential of King. If King could move an audience of 30,000 at the Prayer Pilgrimage, Rustin reasoned, imagine the impact of this charismatic Southern preacher before an even larger audience.

If there was ever a time to march on Washington it was 1963. Although the first march in 1941 never happened, and a youth march in 1959 was not the spectacular event Rustin had hoped for, the third would be the charm.

This time, it would be one of the most unforgettable moments of the twentieth century.

Rustin had disagreed with Randolph about abandoning the 1941 march. Now, he felt vindicated. Every day, as more black and white Americans continued to protest in deep pockets of the south and these protests were broadcast to a national audience of television viewers and written up in newspapers, Rustin knew that the Civil Rights Movement was connecting with people. For his part, Randolph had also thought better of his 1941 decision. While life was better for Pullman porters, many black children were waking up hungry because they'd had no food the previous evening, and would have none while they were in school. Educated men and women were unemployed. Black people still worked for below-standard wages in cotton and tobacco fields. And seeing front page photos of whites pouring ketchup and sugar on the heads of college students trying to integrate lunch counters in the South disturbed him, as it would most people who cannot tolerate injustice. While Randolph was adored by the black community and had earned the respect of three Presidents, he was deeply saddened by the conditions he saw when he traveled the country on behalf of the Brotherhood of Sleeping Car Porters.

But Randolph was a pragmatist. He had called off the 1941 march because he had met a specific goal: to end discrimination in the defense industry. What would the goal of this march be? How could he and Rustin now condense the concerns of black people into a concrete statement that would serve as a call to action? What was the issue that would serve as the battle cry? The march couldn't celebrate a third or seventh anniversary of a legislative victory, but it could inspire legislation. Wasn't the end result of the threatened 1941 march an executive order?

Some civil rights leaders had labeled the Civil Rights Act of 1957 a sham. The original proposal had called for the appointment of "an attorney general for civil rights" who would be "empowered to seek injunctive relief in the federal courts for people whose constitutional rights had been violated," but this provision was stricken.

According to Thomas Gentile's *The March on Washington*, Rustin and Randolph had brought up the idea for the march in December 1962 during a discussion of the "Civil Rights Movement in the South, and their own wish to become active once again in the movement." There they were, remembering great times, victories won, challenges sidelined. After they had finished their stroll down memory lane, they thought about the present and the future. Rustin agreed to "prepare a memo outlining the possibilities and tentative plans for a march."

Just before March1963, Rustin, who had enlisted two young disciples, Norman Hill and Tom Kahn, outlined a plan for an event that would focus on two urgent needs for black people: jobs and equal rights. Rustin's plan originally sought support from the Negro American Labor Council. "It would be a two-day program, a Friday and Saturday in May. Later, it was decided that to effectively plan and gather support for the March it would need to be held in October 1963. The first day of the program was to be dedicated to lobbying at the White House and Congress by labor, church and civil rights leaders. The second day would be the mass march and rally. Support of big labor would be sought as well as the support of some of the other civil rights leaders."

News of a second March on Washington scheduled for the summer soon leaked to the press. There was also a rumor circulating that the "SCLC was making preliminary plans for a march that summer." Randolph, who had been waiting for this for more than two decades, could barely contain himself. But when Randolph told the Negro

American Labor Council of his plans for a March for Jobs on Washington, "the idea seemed to generate little excitement." Perhaps if the Prayer Pilgrimage had been better planned and attended, there would be more enthusiasm for the March on Washington.

All the while, Rustin and Randolph began to exchange memos on a variety of issues, including logistics, transportation, sit-ins, and potential speakers, just in case.

In early March, Randolph decided to make an aggressive move. He suggested June 13 and 14 as a target date for the March on Washington. It would be the two-day conference that he'd wanted. There would be speakers and performers. The masses would sit-in at the chambers of Congress.

Throughout April, Randolph had to scale back his plans when events in Birmingham began to take precedence on the nation's agenda. Randolph had to be careful that he not take attention from the movement, as he was trying to bring all the leaders of various movements together under one tent.

Meanwhile, on May 24, Robert Kennedy's growing sensitivity to civil rights issues was heightened considerably by a contentious meeting in New York with writer James Baldwin, psychologist Kenneth Clark, Lena Horne, the playwright Lorrainne Hansberry, Clarence Jones, Harry Belafonte, and a number of other leading performers and civil rights activists. Those present told Kennedy that his administration was out of touch. They warned him that there would be a mounting crisis if the federal government did not get behind the movement.

Responding to a series of rebellions that began to erupt in poor black neighborhoods, *Newsweek* declared, "Everywhere plain signs arose that Birmingham had thrust the whole U.S. racial problem into a new phase—more intense, more flammable, more urgent ... Among whites, North and South, the crisis not only spurred conscience but touched a nerve of fear."

With the media focused on Birmingham, King knew that the

Civil Rights Movement was foremost on the minds of Americans. Like Roosevelt, he thought that Kennedy should issue an executive order banning all federal discrimination.

In early June, King increased the pressure on Kennedy to propose legislation that would address civil rights. Kennedy was stunned when he learned that King had told audiences that Kennedy was as ineffective as Eisenhower on civil rights. In response, Kennedy hastily pasted together civil rights legislation that he would send to Congress.

On June 11, Kennedy went before the nation with his tour-de-force statement on civil rights. His victory was short-lived. Medgar Evers was assassinated late in the evening.

According to Thomas C. Reeves in *A Question of Character,* "the following week blacks rioted, marched, sat in, or picketed in Savannah, Danville, Virginia, Cambridge, Maryland, New York City, Providence, Rhode Island, and dozens of other cities."

Randolph invited King, Fred Shuttlesworth, and Ralph Abernathy for a meeting in New York on June 18 to discuss, among other issues, a March on Washington.

The next day, Kennedy revealed details for his Civil Rights Act of 1963, which "called for federal authority to grant blacks the right to be served in public places, to attend an integrated school, to receive federally financed training and education, and to look for a job without fear of discrimination."

Publicly, Kennedy put on a brave face, but privately, he thought that the bill would be one of the defining moments of his presidency, and a determining factor in whether he would win re-election. He was concerned about the civil rights leaders' plans and had heard talk of a March on Washington.

On June 20, King was elated by Kennedy's legislation. This was a civil rights bill worth supporting. Knowing that the Southern voting bloc would try to kill the bill, King decided to go on the offensive:

On June 21, March coordinators George Lawrence and Cleveland Robinson, a trade unionist with New York's local District 65, officially announced that there would be a March on Washington "to draw national attention to the problem of [Negro] unemployment and the need for thousands of new jobs, and not simply to lobby for civil rights legislation."

The date was set: Wednesday, August 28, 1963.

The clock was ticking.

JOHN MARSHALL KILIMANJARO REMEMBERS

"It was a special day. We felt like one. If you got lost, you could get on any bus, as long as there was a seat."

When my wife and I arrived at our bus, there was not one black person from Greensboro that I knew. I didn't see any teachers from my wife's school, nor professors from the local colleges. The people I saw were ordinary folks—yardmen, maids, cooks, one or two preachers. None of the big dog preachers that we came to know, were there. Contrary to the mythology, the early moments of the March—getting there—was no picnic. People were afraid. We didn't know what we would meet. There was no precedent. Sitting across from me was a black preacher with a white collar. He was an AME preacher. We talked. Every now and then, people on the bus sang "Oh Freedom" and "We Shall Overcome," but for the most part, there wasn't a whole bunch of singing. We were secretly praying that nothing violent happened.

As we rode out of North Carolina into Virginia—understand that it was still dark outside—it was if the air got cleaner on I-95. We stopped in Virginia to get some gas. There was no one at the rest stop. We walked around a bit to stretch and saw this big mound of earth—it seemed as if there was some construction or building going on. Several of us decided to climb to the top of this mound. It wasn't a hill, but it was steep enough that we saw the need to grab each other's hands. As we got to the top of the mound, the sun was slowly rising, and as we looked out, all we saw were buses, coming from the north, east, west and south. And we knew it was our people. We burst into applause. The thing that we were most afraid of was the March would be a bust. We thought that we were going to let Dr. King down.

When we started out again, we had a new attitude. We weren't as tentative with our emotions. We arrived in Washington, D.C. at 6:45 A.M. We got a seat by the Reflecting Pool. By 11 A.M., the sun was heating up, and folks started fainting and passing out. There were some people who didn't know any better, and jumped in the Reflecting Pool. We made it a regular black thing. Folks were singing songs and making speeches. People were waiting for Dr. King. When he reached those high points, people clapped, and he knew how to hit folks where we knew that he was tailoring things to us, and people got it, and they laughed. When King said, "the Red Sea opened...and we were able to get out of Egypt," using the example of Moses leading the children out of Egypt, we knew that he was talking about George Wallace, and all of those sons of bitches who were determined to hold us back. He made this magnificent speech, and you couldn't hear anything, there was so much applause. It was a special day. We felt like one. If you got lost, you could get on any bus, as long as there was a seat.

The March was certainly a success. When King said 'Go back to Mississippi and go back to your town...' I listened, and acted as soon as I got home.

Dr. King and members of the Big Ten march to the Lincoln Memorial.

CHAPTER 6
BEHIND CLOSED DOORS

When Wilkins walked into the room, about a dozen or so people were
chatting, waiting to take their seats. Wilkins immediately shook his
head and began walking through the room, tapping people on the
shoulder, saying who would stay and who had to leave. These were
powerful people he was ordering around, and he was not very polite.
It was amazing to me that he would do that. Even more amazing
was the fact that the others obeyed.
—John Lewis

In photographs of meetings at the White House, Urban League offices, conventions, press conferences or attending church services, the Big Six—A. Philip Randolph, Roy Wilkins, John Lewis, Whitney Young, Martin Luther King, Jr., and James Farmer—exude confidence.

Increasingly, these six powerful men lived in two worlds: the political and the personal, one white, in which they were still strangers but becoming increasingly familiar with its insider/outsider rules; the other, black, where they were treated as extended members of the family. In this realm, they'd spoken at countless programs, greeted children, comforted widowed mothers, delivered sermons, danced, shared stories, recited prayers, and broke bread. And now, as they moved between these two very different worlds, they had to confront unique challenges and opportunities.

With less than eight weeks remaining before the March, outside pressures and in-group tensions were mounting. Some situations were unavoidable, some unexplainable. Strained relations between members that had been simmering for months now reached the boiling point. There were old unsettled rivalries, and new ones were forming. For the next two months, the leaders would disagree, fall out, and fall back into place.

As civil rights leaders, they understood that internal and external scrutiny was a part of the package. Now, however, there was concern that their phones were tapped. Their lives were under public examination. They were treading on unfamiliar territory.

The announcement of the March was the easy part. Now came the work. There were a number of hurdles to confront and overcome. Whatever conflicts the group had to face, individually or collectively, would have to be set aside for the greater good of the March and to ensure that Kennedy's proposed civil rights bill would clear every obstacle presented in Congress.

Several leaders lamented that they hadn't received attention from Kennedy, but that quickly changed. After the announcement of the March on Washington, they were moved from back-burner to front-burner status with the President.

Kennedy was angered by the announcement. Concerned that a march on Washington by thousands of Negroes would not only delay progress for civil rights legislation, he knew that such an action could adversely impact several bills that were in session, including an education and tax-reduction package. He was worried for other reasons as well: After his June 12 speech advocating a civil rights bill, his poll numbers dipped below fifty percent.

On June 22, A. Philip Randolph, Roy Wilkins, Martin Luther King, Jr., John Lewis, and others met at the White House to discuss establishing a Leadership Conference on Civil Rights. Kennedy wanted their advice on the civil rights bill.

As author Thomas Gentile describes the meeting in *The March on Washington*, Kennedy wastes no time in chiding the group for announcing the March. He questions the wisdom of staging it when civil rights was in its infancy.

"We want success in Congress, not just a big show at the Capitol," said the President. "Some of these people are looking for an excuse to be against us. I don't want to give any of them a chance to say, 'Yes, I'm for the bill, but I'll be damned if I will vote for it at the point of a gun.' It seemed to me a great mistake to announce a march on Washington before the bill was even in committee. The only effect is to create an atmosphere of intimidation—and this may give some members of Congress an out."

"The Negroes are already in the streets," said A. Philip Randolph. "There *will* be a march."

Citing Birmingham, King mentioned that there was "no perfect time for civil unrest."

Without missing a beat, Kennedy responded:

"I don't think you should all be totally harsh on Bull Connor. After all, he has done more for civil rights than anybody else."

Kennedy's remark was stinging, partially because it was unexpected, but mainly because through a politician's eyes, it was the truth.

If the children of Birmingham gained international compassion after they were sprayed with fire hoses and bitten by dogs, Police Commissioner T. Eugene "Bull" Connor hardened hearts with his aggressive behavior. Wielding a police stick and a grimace, Connor often mentioned in press reports that he was upholding the law— which caused many people to question the law. From Maine to Moscow, Bull Connor was seen as a symbol of segregation.

Having looked into Connor's eyes, some of the men felt the sting of Kennedy's comment. That was the intent. Kennedy understood the ugly side of politics. Most in the room were religious and civic leaders. In 1963, there were only five black members of Congress: Adam Clayton Powell from Harlem, William Dawson from Chicago, Augustus Hawkins from Los Angeles, Charles Diggs from Detroit, and Robert N.C. Nix from Philadelphia. Among them, perhaps Powell, a master politician, could have understood the coldness of Kennedy's remark, and probably would have expected it.

Kennedy's response alerted the leaders that the stakes had risen. They were no longer in rural and city churches, delivering rousing speeches and raising funds. Washington may have been miles from

Birmingham, Alabama; Rock Hill, South Carolina, and Nashville, Tennessee, but its network of power brokers and deal makers was just as Byzantine as those in the smaller cities. The group had to remember that the laws that they were challenging were the same laws that delivered many white politicians to Washington.

Before the group could recover from his statement, Kennedy ended the meeting and invited King for a stroll in the Rose Garden. There, he told King that the FBI was concerned about King's colleagues Stanley Levison and Jack O'Dell and their affiliation with the SCLC. Both Burke Marshall and Robert Kennedy had tried to warn King that Levison not only had Communist sympathies, but, was, in fact, a Communist himself. King dismissed the accusation. The FBI claimed that there was ample evidence to suggest that both Levison and O'Dell were Communists. They had wiretapped Levison's phone. Marshall and Robert Kennedy insinuated that Levison was a powerful operative who had infiltrated the Civil Rights Movement to cause chaos and to destroy the United States government.

King was steadfast in his support of Levison, a white attorney who had been one of King's staunchest allies. Bayard Rustin had introduced King to Levison when Rustin became interested in the Montgomery bus boycotts. Rustin and Levison were both members of In Friendship, which raised funds for the fledgling Civil Rights Movement. King had now known Levison for at least eight years. Levison had been instrumental in the publishing of King's book, *Stride Toward Freedom.* As David J. Garrow makes clear in *Bearing the Cross: Martin Luther King, Jr. and the Southern Christian Leadership Conference,* both Levison and Jack O'Dell, a black attorney, had been highly effective in raising funds for the SCLC. Indeed, their most recent "efforts produced a list of nine thousand proven contributors, individuals who could be counted on to support SCLC at least twice a year." Kennedy warned King that if he continued his relationship with Levison, it would be at his own peril. King knew that there was much at stake, not just the March on Washington, but the Civil Rights

Bill, and although he didn't say it, King knew his reputation would be harmed. King, who was known for his loyalty, was in a dilemma. He said he would not respond unless there was evidence to support the allegation. According to Garrow, "This notice put Robert Kennedy and Burke Marshall into a stall, [since] they could not fulfill the promise to King without violating their duty to protect Hoover's secrets."

But as Diane McWhorter reveals in *Carry Me Home, Birmingham, Alabama: The Climactic Battle of the Civil Rights Revolution,* "on June 30, the *Birmingham News* revealed that O'Dell, was a suspected Communist, who was still on [the] SCLC's payroll." Levison, anticipating the same bad press, distanced himself from the movement for fear that he would harm the cause. He and King began communicating through Clarence Jones.

King and members of the SCLC were concerned about the FBI and the prospect of wiretaps. And they had other headaches as well: calming their own internal conflicts. There had been tension between King and Wilkins for some time, but in truth, the real source was Wilkins. Since its founding in 1909, the NAACP had been considered the nation's premier civil rights organization, and in 1963, its leader Roy Wilkins was seen as a spokesperson for Negro Americans. Now, the NAACP's preeminent role was in question. Some thought that the group was too conservative. The SCLC and SNCC were the new powers in the Civil Rights Movement. It was a perceived battle of the old versus the new. Publicly, King and Wilkins were highly complimentary of each other, but privately, things were not the same. Wilkins' cool elegance was at times undone by his own pointed, sharp manner. Garrow notes that Wilkins "complained about King's alleged presumptuousness and self-promoting to anyone who would listen Wilkins still reminded King that he owed his early fame to the NAACP lawsuit that had settled the Montgomery bus boycott, and he still taunted King for being young, naïve, and ineffectual, saying that King's methods had not integrated a single classroom in Albany or

Birmingham."

When King asked Wilkins to put together a memorial fund for Medgar Evers, Wilkins is reported to have told King to "mind his own business." After the June 22 meeting with Kennedy, when Wilkins was asked about the March, he replied:

"That baby does not belong to me."

* * *

On July 2, the leaders met at New York's Roosevelt Hotel to outline their plans for the March.

Strong minded and bristly, Wilkins was known to not only ruffle feathers, but to pluck nerves. Few knew that he had survived a bout of stomach cancer in 1946, and had been left with a gall bladder problem. But the cancer made him no less effective. Outspoken and opinionated, he was both feared and respected. And when he walked into the dining room at the Roosevelt Hotel, he was not in a great mood. He immediately took umbrage at the place settings for fifteen people, and began to point to individuals, suggesting who could remain and who should remove themselves from the room.

Nine people left the room—including Fred Shuttlesworth, Norman Hill, Cleveland Robinson, and Bayard Rustin.

Rustin's expulsion came as a major surprise. He was viewed by everyone in the room, with the exception of Wilkins (and perhaps Whitney Young of the Urban League), as the natural director of the March. No one had Rustin's organizational skills, experience, connections or the passion he brought to dealing with major and minor details of the March.

"Look, Bayard," Wilkins reportedly said. "I want you to know that I'm not in favor of your organizing the March on Washington."

Rustin knew he was viewed by many as controversial. He was a conscientious objector during the war, and had been labeled a draft dodger. Although he was a Socialist, people equated him with a

Communist, since he had belonged to the Young Communist League. And he had been brought up on a California sex charge.

But Rustin was solid in his commitment to civil rights. He had taken part in a 1947 bus protest, the "Journey of Reconciliation," which attempted to desegregate interstate bus facilities in the South. He was a visionary. Rustin believed that the Montgomery movement could bring wider attention to national civil rights, and recommended the establishment of workshops on nonviolence.

Roy Wilkins understood Rustin's contributions to the movement, but was resolute in his opinion that Rustin should not be the director of the March.

Wilkins, himself, wasn't free of scandal. There were rumors that Wilkins was working on behalf of the Kennedys, not the movement. But in the end, Wilkins got his way—with a compromise. Randolph was appointed director of the March and Randolph chose Rustin as deputy director.

Bayard Rustin proudly hung out a sign from the third-story window of March headquarters on West 130th Street: March on Washington for Jobs and Freedom—August 28. In *Parting the Waters*, Taylor Branch recalls that "the weathered stucco building was owned by the Friendship Baptist Church of the Rev. Thomas Kilgore—Ella Baker's pastor, a King family friend almost from the time of King's birth."

Like the March efforts, the headquarters was a work in progress. "There was no elevator, a hand-lettered sign directed visitors to walk upstairs to the office, where Rustin, in a cloud of cigarette smoke, raced incessantly between telephones and borrowed typewriters. He had less than sixty days to devise plans to mobilize, transport, service and control some 100,000 human bodies."

As Randolph and every leader around the table at the Roosevelt Hotel knew, Rustin was the right man for the job. According to Gentile, "within two weeks he had distributed his Organizing Manual No. 1 to two thousand interested leaders."

But it was still too early to measure whether his efforts were registering in black communities.

On July 17, Kennedy dropped his opposition to the March. At a press conference, he "endorsed the peaceful assembly, calling for a redress of grievances. 'I think [the March on Washington] is in the great tradition.' He added that he looked forward to attending the event, and declared, 'This is not a march on the Capitol.'"

Meanwhile, the civil rights bill was moving from the back burner to the front burner on the nation's legislative docket. On Capitol Hill, through mid-July, the Senate Commerce Committee held hearings on the administration's civil rights bill.

Alabama Governor George Wallace, in an effort to undermine the March, not only showed his contempt for the bill, but also suggested that the bill and the movement were anti-American.

"As a loyal American and as a loyal Southern Governor who has never belonged to or associated with any subversive element, I resent the fawning and pawing over such people as Martin Luther King and his pro-Communist associates," Wallace said.

These kinds of public comments were countered with articulate and moving speeches from seasoned orators like Roy Wilkins. Wilkins had some detractors in the movement, but no one could doubt his commitment to the cause. He had risen to the heights of his power within the black community because of his charisma and leadership ability. When he spoke before the Senate Commerce Committee, his words sent a chill throughout the chambers of Congress:

For millions of Americans this is vacation time. Families load their automobiles and trek across the country. I invite the members of this committee to imagine themselves darker in color and to plan an auto trip from Norfolk, Virginia, to the Gulf Coast of Mississippi. How far would you drive each day? Where and under what conditions can you and your family eat? Where can they use a restroom? Can you stop after a reasonable day behind the wheel, or must you drive until you reach a city where relatives or friends will accommodate you for the night? Will your children be denied a soft drink or an ice cream cone because they are not white? The Negro American has been waiting upon voluntary action since 1876. He has found what other Americans have discovered: Voluntary action has to be sparked by something stronger than prayers, patience and lamentations...

Wilkins' comments reverberated throughout the black community—though it was unclear what the impact was. Hobbled by a lingering recession and high unemployment, there was a growing restlessness in black communities, particularly in big cities such as New York, Newark, Los Angeles and Chicago. Followers of Elijah Muhammad and the Black Muslim movement subscribed to a self-help doctrine. Whereas the SCLC and SNCC movements relied heavily on nonviolence, the Muslims were not nearly as tolerant.

King condemned their eye-for-an-eye, tooth-for-a-tooth stand. Muslims believed that King underestimated the black community's increased impatience and intolerance of racism.

Far from assuming a separatist stance, March organizers reached out to white leaders in the religious and labor communities. In early August, A. Philip Randolph announced that the six-man black leadership had been supplemented by four white figures—Mathew Ahmann, executive director of the National Catholic Conference of Interracial Justice; Dr. Eugene Carson Blacke, vice chairman of the Commission on Race Relations of the National Council of Churches of Christ in America; Rabbi Joachim Prinz, president of the American Jewish Congress; and Walter Reuther, president of the United Auto Workers trade union. During the announcement, Randolph called for Kennedy to accept his offer to attend the March.

The interracial Big Ten had its complications. Anna Arnold Hedgeman, the lone woman on the board, recalled in her memoir that when "television crews came to the headquarters of the National Urban League, the committee had their pictures taken, without the white members."

On August 3, organizers met in Harlem for a progress report from

Rustin. In Gentile's account, "the budget for the March had ballooned from $65,000 to $75,000. The last youth march, in 1959, had only cost $34,000. Although thirty thousand dollars in new contributions had come in from churches, individuals and labor unions, more money was still needed. Leaders were asked to redouble their efforts. The March could not be a disappointment. And March leaders were now under pressure from the Kennedy administration to make sure that all logistics would be handled carefully so that the city would not erupt into chaos."

During the most intense hours of preparation for the March, "burglars broke into the headquarters, stealing petty cash obtained from button sales, postage stamps, and five Royal typewriters."

Directors and their deputies were encouraged to go into overdrive to insure a successful turnout. Rustin was certain that there would be at least "2,000 buses carrying 45 people a piece; 21 special trains each carrying 1,000 people; and 10 airplanes carrying 50 persons each—a total of 11,000. The special trains were coming mostly from New York City and the South, but also from Newark, Philadelphia, Hartford, Pittsburgh, Detroit, Chicago, Cleveland, Minneapolis, and Boulder, Colorado. Boston's contingent would be coming by an all-night bus. Each bus was to have a bus captain who was to carry a complete list of the names of the passengers on his or her bus. Roll was to be called on the trip down, and again prior to starting back from Washington."

The week beginning August 19—the last full week before the March—was highly charged. White House Press Secretary Pierre Salinger confirmed that President Kennedy would not address the rally, but that he would meet with the March leaders sometime during the day. Privately, according to Thomas C. Reeves in *A Question of Character: A Life of John F. Kennedy,* the President "felt that he would be booed at the March, and also didn't want to meet with organizers before the March because he didn't want a list of demands. He arranged a 5 P.M. meeting at the White House with the 10 leaders on the 28th."

On the same day, James Farmer of CORE was arrested in Plaquemine, Louisiana, and jailed along with 16 other demonstrators marching in support of a voter registration drive. He would miss the March.

The next day, President Kennedy held a news conference confirming that he would not address the demonstrators on August 28. Kennedy was not the only important member of the government who would not attend the March. Southern members of Congress not only declined an invitation to attend the March, but also went so far as to let March members know why they would not be present. Senator Olin D. Johnston of South Carolina replied:

"I positively will not attend. You are committing the worst possible mistake in promoting this March. You should know that criminal, fanatical, and communistic elements, as well as crackpots, will move in to take every advantage of this mob. You certainly will have no influence on any member of Congress, including myself."

Rustin went over the last minute details. According to *Time*, he handed out "volley after volley of handbooks, bulletins, press releases, charts, schedules, visceral warnings, and soul-stirring exhortations." The March would begin at the Washington Monument and end at the Lincoln Memorial. Organizers urged "marchers to bring plenty of water, but no 'alcoholic beverages.' They suggested peanut butter and jelly sandwiches. They reminded everyone to wear low-heeled shoes, to bring a raincoat, to wear a hat, to remember their sunglasses. They told marchers to leave their children at home, and strongly suggested that each marcher buy a 25 cents button, displaying a black hand clasping a white hand and wear it on parade. They arranged for 292 outdoor toilets, 21 portable water fountains, 22 first aid stations manned by 40 doctors and 80 nurses to be scattered under the monument and along the route to the march."

They finalized the speakers for the day. Among them: Reverend Patrick O'Boyle, Archbishop of Washington, who would do the invocation; A. Philip Randolph, who would act as a master of ceremonies and provide the opening remarks; Daisy Bates, who would offer a Tribute to Negro Women Fighters for Freedom; and John Lewis, national chairman of the Student Nonviolent Coordinating Committee.

Next up would be Walter Reuther , President, United Automobile, Aerospace and Agricultural Implement Workers, Chairman, AFL-CIO, Chairman, Industrial Union Department, AFL-CIO; James Farmer, National Director, Congress of Racial Equality; Rabbi Uri Miller, President, Synagogue Council of America; Whitney M. Young, Jr., Executive Director, National Urban League; Mathew Ahmann, Executive Director, National Catholic Conference for Interracial Justice; Roy Wilkins, Executive Secretary, for the National Association for the Advancement of Colored People; Rabbi Joachim Prinz, President, American Jewish Congress; and Dr. Martin Luther King, Jr., President, Southern Christian Leadership Conference.

Randolph would lead the Pledge of Allegiance, and Dr. Benjamin E. Mays, President, Morehouse College, would lead the benediction. In between, there would be musical numbers from Marian Anderson, who would sing The National Anthem, plus Eva Jessye, and Mahalia Jackson.

Rustin warned the speakers that "a hook man would unceremoniously yank them from the podium if their speeches exceeded seven minutes. He was determined to move the huge mass of people into Washington after dawn and out again before dusk, and therefore he could not tolerate the usual stretch of performers' egos."

Speakers had to submit their speeches to organizers for approval. Patrick O'Boyle took offense with John Lewis' remarks.

According to *Time*, Lewis' original draft suggested that "Kennedy's civil rights package was too little and too late. 'Listen, Mr. Kennedy. Listen, Mr. Congressman. Listen, fellow citizens. The black masses are on the March for jobs and freedom. We will march through the South, through the heart of Dixie, the way Sherman did. We shall pursue our own scorched-earth policy."

The initial draft also included a section of the civil rights bill that required men and women to have at least a sixth-grade education to be able to register to vote. Lewis saw a photograph in *The New York Times* with a group of Rhodesian women holding signs that said, "One Man, One Vote," and decided to use it. He implied that lovers of freedom would "keep pushing and keep moving."

Time said that after "Washington's Roman Catholic Archbishop Patrick O'Boyle saw an advance copy of the Lewis speech, he considered it an incitement to riot, and refused to deliver an invocation to the ceremonies unless Lewis agreed to tone it down."

The morning of the March, behind Lincoln's statue, controversy about Lewis' speech would erupt, although he promised the group that he had made the requisite changes.

A. Philip Randolph, the voice of reason, pulled Lewis aside:

"I have waited twenty-two years for this," Randolph said. "I've waited all my life for this opportunity. Please don't ruin it. John, we've come this far together. Let us stay together."

As he would take his turn on the podium, Lewis' speech would be modified, but was no less powerful.

*The magnificent Marian Anderson performs a solo
at the March on Washington.*

Reverend Abraham Woods Remembers

*"I caught the freedom train in Florida that would arrive in
Washington. The train from Florida was my pride and joy.
The coaches would pick up people in Georgia, the Carolinas,
Virginia, and then we would arrive in Washington, D.C.
We were concerned whether there would be incidents, so every-
one was encouraged to be on their best behavior.
When the train pulled into Union Station, we saw buses
coming from everywhere filled with people.
I'm telling you, we were just elated."*

I was surprised when I received a call asking me to go to
Atlanta and work out of Dr. King's office as Dr. King's
Deputy Director for the March on Washington. Dr. C.K.
Steele, one of the vice-presidents, and one of the founding
leaders of the SCLC in Tallahassee, Florida started a bus boycott there, and he was responsible for me getting the call. He
had been to Birmingham and had spoken at the Sixteenth
Street Church. I had to coordinate all of the activities for the
Southeast: pulling the buses, the trains and car pools together. This really intensified in June. I traveled around the South
to various cities, speaking to the leaders, encouraging everyone to charter as many buses as they could to be a part of the
freedom train. I received great assistance from the national
organization and the SCLC. I was concentrated in places like
Georgia, Alabama, and Mississippi, and Florida, and Virginia.
We would travel to New York almost weekly for meetings
with the Urban League, Whitney Young and labor and religious leaders, and we would give our reports.

Everyone was concerned about the crowd. Politicians
didn't count. If we didn't have the crowd, it would be perceived that we would've flunked. That drove us to work even

harder. We wanted to make sure that a lot of people were there. I wrote to Southern leaders, and I had them meet with me at the SCLC headquarters. In late July, things started to come together. The day before the March was hectic. I caught the freedom train in Florida that would arrive in Washington. The train from Florida was my pride and joy. The coaches would pick up people in Georgia, the Carolinas, Virginia, and then we would arrive in Washington, D.C. We were concerned whether there would be incidents, so everyone was encouraged to be on their best behavior. When the train pulled into Union Station, we saw buses coming from everywhere filled with people. I'm telling you, we were just elated. Endless lines of buses coming. We were happy, overjoyed. We knew then that the people were heeding the call. And the March was going to be the greatest ever.

I had the advantage of sitting in the VIP section, standing some distance behind King, and in front of Lincoln in his chair. I saw people in the woods, in the Reflecting Pool. It looked like more than a quarter of a million people. I was surprised by the final count. It seemed very conservative. A. Philip Randolph was very eloquent. I'm telling you, when he spoke he spoke with a great sense of authority. He did the introductions. I remember John Lewis' speech. They sort of toned him down. His speech would've been more radical than it was. "The Tribute to the Women" was special.

The singing of Mahalia Jackson was just amazing. King's speech was remarkable. Everybody was ecstatic about the March. That's all you could hear was about the March. We won a victory by the demonstrations. We got many of the things that we wanted. The lunch counters were desegregated. People placed in jails had their charges dropped. No more black water, white water fountains. When we returned home, we knew that the Birmingham schools had to be desegregated.

On September 10, 1963, a school in Birmingham was desegregated, and one of my colleagues, James Armstrong sought to put one of his children in the school. And then five days later, on September 15, 1963, the Sixteenth Street Baptist Church was bombed...

Over the past forty years, Birmingham has had many positive changes. We didn't feel like City Hall belonged to us as citizens. Now, we've had black mayors, black city council members, black police and fire chiefs, black judges, black superintendent, and blacks serving in various capacities in city hall and in the county. But over the years, many whites moved out of the city. The schools now have a ninety percent black student body. But whites are fifty percent of the faculty. Everything has changed. And when you look at it, nothing has changed. Racism is under the surface, and an incident that could scratch it, can bring it out. One would have to be an ostrich to say that there is no more racism.

Blacks seem to have lost their sense of direction, we find ourselves exposed. I know Dr. King is turning in his grave about this black on black homicide. So many blacks have gotten addicted to drugs. So many of our young people are carrying babies, when they should be carrying books. Dr. King didn't die for that. The KKK or skinheads are our enemies, but we're killing ourselves. Many people don't care about the civil rights struggle. During the bombing trials here, there were more whites attending than blacks. I'm very disappointed at what has happened in the black community.

People are not ashamed about anything now. Crime is escalating. Some of this is laid at the door of drug use. Priorities and lifestyles are going to have to be changed. I'm preaching harder. There has to be some change or hope will be lost. We are our brother's keeper.

"This is our moment."

Chapter 7

THE WOMEN

*During these hectic times while we are fighting for human dignity,
and many times for survival, one forgets the contributions
made by women.*
—Daisy Bates

In the bus boycotts and freedom rides, the sit-ins and school desegregation, in voters' registration drives and other ways, women's contributions have been critical to the movement's success. Women not only enhanced the movement—as leaders and supporters—but in many ways, they defined it. There was no situation, request, or detail too great or too small that they did not address, more often than not, to perfection.

In particular, "women laid the foundation for and built the organizational infrastructure that was used to conduct legal challenges, boycotts, voter registration, and other direct actions, including the most intense phases of the campaign that led to the passage of civil rights legislation," says Dianne Pinderhughes in *Black Women in America: A Historical Encyclopedia*.

They designed picket signs, sold buttons, and raised funds through bake sales. Between cooking and cleaning (sometimes their homes and others), choir rehearsals, club meetings, and church—mothers, wives, daughters, attorneys, domestics, journalists, doctors, nurses, sharecroppers, social workers and teachers—typed memos, reports, and newsletters, drove car-pools, and organized meetings to plot movement strategy.

"The black woman's sense of community was a powerful force in this time of crisis," wrote Dr. Darlene Clark Hine and Kathleen Thompson in *A Shining Thread of Hope*. "So, too, was her sense of the efficacy of even small actions. These women who had founded schools and hospitals by running bake sales and quilting bees were in a direct line politically from Dr. Mary McLeod Bethune, who bought the land for her school by selling pies and ended up an advisor of presidents. Others might view the early stirrings of the movement with cynicism and despair, but black women knew better. And if their names were not household names, that was no big surprise. They knew just how much you can get done if you don't care about who gets the credit."

In fact as Pinderhughes recalls, "the women who founded and joined Delta Sigma Theta and Alpha Kappa Alpha sororities, the National Association of Colored Women (NACW), the National Council of Negro Women, the Alpha Suffrage Club in Chicago, local Parent-Teacher Associations, the Independent Order of St. Luke in Richmond, and the Young Women's Christian Association (YWCA), also founded local chapters of the NAACP and the Urban League in cities and towns throughout the South."

They were everyday women and foot soldiers for the movement. Some shelled peas, picked cotton, and plucked chickens. Others held court over afternoon teas and ate finger sandwiches while they played bridge. Some were glamorous; some liked getting their hands dirty. They often took a backseat to the men. They typed and edited the speeches that the men read. They prepared lavish spreads of home-cooked food for critical strategy sessions. They cleaned up after all was said, done, and eaten.

They whispered powerful prayers and sang mighty hymns when their husbands, sons, fathers and pastors were in jeopardy, and they, too, were spat upon, called vile names, jailed, assaulted, and even murdered.

Whether from the South like Rosa Parks, Myrlie Evers, Ella Baker and Fannie Lou Hamer, or the Midwest like Diane Nash Bevel, or the North like Constance Baker Motley and Anna Arnold Hedgeman, individually and collectively, they were unafraid to challenge the status quo. And in Hedgeman's case, to not only challenge opponents of the movement, but even the most powerful black leaders in the nation, who in 1963 were on the Administrative Committee of the March on Washington.

On Friday, August 16, 1963, a final meeting was called in New York City for the Administrative Committee of the March on Washington. Ostensibly, the meeting would solve such last-minute challenges as a lack of buses, parking problems, the sound system and accommodations. It was business as usual, at least for the eighteen men who attended.

But for Anna Arnold Hedgeman, the lone woman on the committee (Rachelle Horowitz oversaw transportation for the group but was not on the central committee), the meeting was something more. During the group's previous session, when the final program was presented for review, Hedgeman was outraged to discover that no woman would speak. She was further aggrieved that a "solution" to recognize women involved A. Philip Randolph's "Tribute to Women," a singling out of various black women in the struggle, who would stand as he spoke. These women—leaders, educators, pioneers—would remain standing as Randolph continued to speak about their role in the movement. Once he ended, the women would bow or nod, and then take their seat. Men choreographed this moment. Women would have no say-so. They would have no voice.

Hedgeman was devastated.

Throughout the planning of the March, Hedgeman proposed that leaders of women's organizations, including the National Association of Colored Women's Clubs, the National Council of Negro Women, the women's sororities and fraternal organization be added to the Committee. They deserved it, she said, given the visibility and importance of Rosa Parks, Daisy Bates, and Myrlie Evers, who, as the wife of the first martyr of the movement, demonstrated amazing grace and dignity. In her autobiography *The Trumpet Sounds: A Memoir of Negro Leadership* Hedgeman surmised, that as usual, "the men must have discussed the matter in [her] absence." The first time that she'd heard about the limited role of women at the March, she was "embarrassed."

According to Lynne Olson in *Freedom's Daughters,* "from the start, [Hedgeman] had objected to the way the March's leaders regarded women. She didn't like that she was the only woman on the planning committee, but her fellow members ignored her complaints about that, just as they later ignored her objections to the invisibility of women in the March. In her view, the last-minute 'Tribute to Women' didn't come close to recognition. [But] at the same time, she didn't want to make a big fuss, didn't want to embarrass Wilkins, Randolph, and the rest."

Hedgeman had patiently waited for the men of the committee to do the honorable thing. When that failed, she decided to take matters into her own hands and talk to Corinne Smith and Geri Stark, who, together had raised more than $14,000 for the March as members of the Negro American Labor Council. In her memoir, Hedgeman reveals that when she told the women about the glaring omission of anyone to represent them on the dais, they "were even more disturbed than [she] had anticipated." Smith was adamant that "a woman ought to be on that program." Hedgeman was moved. She pondered what it would mean not to have a woman speak, and then began thinking of great black women leaders who had inspired her.

Hedgeman, whose significant contributions to civil and women's rights are often overlooked, had been making the case for women and Negroes for most of her sixty-four years. She'd spent "most of her life as an administrator in predominantly white institutions—the YWCA, the federal government, and the administration of New York Mayor Robert Wagner—and in each job, she had been an outspoken champion of racial and social justice."

Her political and personal connections were numerous, her reputation, impeccable. She was an advisor and great friend to A. Philip Randolph. In fact, Randolph called on Hedgeman in the fall of 1962, when he was trying to build a coalition of Muslims, black nationalists, and Puerto Ricans to work together on social and economic unity. The group never came together because it couldn't get support from benefactors. Undaunted, in early February, Randolph suggested to Hedgeman that they should start thinking beyond benefactors.

"We have negotiated long enough about these problems," Randolph said. "The people must move, for only the people can produce the change we must have." While he had discussed the March on Washington with Rustin in December 1962, he shared his idea with Hedgeman the following February.

Hedgeman recalls that hearing about the March left her with a sense of excitement. She felt that the March on Washington "might well be a way of giving young people a new picture of their leadership and a new sense of their dignity. Present in the meeting that day was Richard Parrish, who as a leader of Negro teachers had been struggling against limitations of the white-dominated school system for two decades, and Hope Stevens, an attorney and active supporter of Negro job opportunity."

An official meeting to discuss the March on Washington would take place a week later. Randolph had told Hedgeman that the March would happen in October. At the same time, Hedgeman came across a quote from King and members of the SCLC that mentioned a march on Washington.

Hedgeman "clipped the article from [the newspaper] and went to see Randolph." She suggested that he and Martin Luther King should begin immediate conversations about "the amalgamation of their plans." Randolph relented. With the aid of Martin's brother (the Rev. B.D. King), Randolph and Martin Luther King, Jr. agreed to work together to develop the idea of a March on Washington for Jobs and Freedom, with October mentioned as a possible date.

March for what? Hedgeman's mind was filled with ideas. Talking with Smith and Stark, she thought deeply about the importance of having a voice, and she "talked of the tragedy of the Negro slave woman, of the heroic leadership of women like Harriet Tubman and Sojourner Truth as well as Rosa Parks." She stopped talking and put her thoughts to paper. She wrote a letter to "Mr. Randolph," and sent copies to him and the other leaders in anticipation of the August 16 meeting.

Hedgeman's letter was strongly worded, but sensible. As the nine-teen-member committee met to discuss last minute details, Hedgeman waited patiently for the moment that she would speak. There she was, the lone woman in the room, who had performed mir-acles for the March. Hedgeman had worked with more than 30,000 white Protestants from across the nation and encouraged them to bring buses to Washington. She worked "with the Council of Churches and organizations of church women and men in every state, asking them to arrange consultations and demonstrations in their cities and to mobilize participants who could come to Washington."

As the meeting neared adjournment, Hedgeman realized that her letter would not be addressed. The "Tribute to Women" would go on as proposed.

She drew upon her inner resources, stood, and read her letter aloud:

In light of the role of Negro women in the struggle for freedom and especially in light of the extra burden they have carried because of the castration of our Negro men in this culture, it is incredible that no woman should appear as a speaker at the historic March on Washington Meeting at the Lincoln Memorial . . .

Since the Big Six have not given women the quality of participation, which they have earned through the years, I would like to make the fol-lowing suggestion:

That a Negro woman makes a brief statement and presents the other Heroines just as you have suggested that the Chairman might do...

It has occurred to me that no woman or man could object to Mrs. Medgar Evers, the widow of our freedom Martyr, for this role. Her per-formance on television just after the murder of her husband proves her ability to make [even] one sentence memorable.

If for some reason the 'Big Six' is unwilling to select Mrs. Evers for this role, it occurs to me that pride in our Militant Younger Generation might make it possible for the older women to bow to youth and ask Mrs. Diane Nash Bevel to represent women and all youth in one person. Recently, Mrs. Bevel told the story of the Negro freedom struggle to the Council of Episcopal Bishops from across the country. She was perceptive, articulate and honest. She is a disciplined person and would observe the time allotted her. Mrs. Bevel is in essence the consummation of the quality of the past of Negro woman and part of the hope of all of us for the future.

If you believe that a poll of Negro women should be made, I shall be pleased as the woman member of the Administrative Committee to accept the responsibility.

I hope that this memorandum will receive careful consideration and submit it in the belief that my service to the 'March Idea,' since you suggested it early in 1963 when you proposed the March for Jobs in October, has been of the quantity and quality which merits reasonable recognition of my proposal.

For a room of, arguably, some of the most loquacious men of their time, the silence was palpable. And then Wilkins spoke.

"No one can quarrel with that statement," he said. "I think the case is made."

The committee settled on a making a "Tribute to Negro Women Fighters for Freedom." Myrlie Evers would introduce Daisy Bates, Diane Nash Bevel, Mrs. Herbert Lee, Rosa Parks, and Gloria Richardson.

Daisy Lee Gatson Bates and her husband L. C. Bates owned and operated the *Arkansas State Press*, the largest and most influential black paper in the state. As president of the Arkansas State Conference of NAACP branches, Bates not only advised nine black schoolchildren during the tumultuous integration of Little Rock's Central High School 1957, but she became a counselor and den mother, and a role model to thousands of black children who sought out women like Bates in their communities.

Diane Nash Bevel was bold. She led the sit-in movement of Nashville students in 1960 to desegregate lunch counters and bus stations. She organized freedom rides. She secured a "reputation as one of the most daring young firebrands in the movement," after she served a "month-long stint in jail" along with three other members of the Student Nonviolent Coordinating Committee (including Ruby Doris Smith of Spelman College) for sitting-in at a drugstore in Rock Hill, South Carolina.

Each of these women had a special and brave story to tell.

On December 1, 1955, Rosa Parks was thinking about an NAACP workshop that she would attend over the weekend as she was waiting for a five o'clock bus to take her home. When she refused to give her seat to a white woman, as it was the law in Montgomery to do, she was arrested and started what some have come to call the Negro Revolution. In response, the black community of Montgomery boycotted public buses, developing an intricate system of car pools, and more often than not, walking miles from their jobs to their homes, through wet weather or under a sweltering sun. A year later, the Supreme Court ruled that Alabama's segregation laws were unconstitutional.

Seven years later, Hedgeman saw Parks in a hotel where she was staying. Hedgeman was struck by how delicate Parks was, both in features and gestures. And she was also moved by Parks' steely determination. "I was conscious of the fact that this quiet, gentle woman would show more clearly than any words of mine, how terrible a civilization must be which would make Rosa Parks leave her seat that a white woman might sit."

Gloria Richardson "broke all the rules" as the leader of the Cambridge, Maryland demonstrations in the spring of 1963. "In a movement where women tended to exert authority behind the scenes, she was unmistakably out front—the head of the only major grassroots campaign beyond the borders of the South. At a time when most local movements were focused on the right to vote and access to public accommodations, Richardson wanted to end racial discrimination in housing, education, and hiring."

Although she was born a daughter of a privileged family in Cambridge, Richardson, a divorced mother of two, and a college graduate, had to work in a garment factory. She was an unrelenting activist for the black community of Cambridge, and was one of the few women at the time who could raise the ire of both "the white power brokers of Cambridge, or Kennedy administration officials, or some of her fellow civil rights leaders."

Mrs. Herbert Lee was widowed when her husband, a farmer and member of the NAACP, was shot and killed by E.H. Hurst, a white politician in Liberty, Mississippi on September 25, 1961. Hurst claimed that he shot Lee in self-defense, but Lewis Allen, who was also black, witnessed the slaying and said it was an act in cold blood. Before he could testify in court, Allen, too, was murdered. Hurst was later acquitted.

The dignity of the widow Lee, standing with her children at her husband's funeral, was unforgettable.

These women inspired thousands of Americans to do their part, in whatever way they could, to advance the cause of civil rights. They had raised funds and consciousness, quietly, and often without credit.

* * *

A few days before the March, organizers discovered that Myrlie Evers had committed to a speaking engagement in Boston, and would miss the event. Daisy Bates was asked to say a few words during the "Tribute to Women."

On the Monday before the March, a brouhaha developed over A. Philip Randolph's scheduled address to the prestigious but all-male National Press Club.

"The Press club luncheons had always been off-limits to female reporters and there were to be no exceptions made. Women reporters were free to observe only from the balcony. Elsie Carper, president of the Women's National Press Club, was livid:

"It is ludicrous and at the same time distressing that a group fighting for civil rights had chosen a private and segregated club to discuss the March for Jobs and Freedom."

Randolph apologized, but he addressed the group anyway.

The women who stood on the podium the day of the March, would see wives, mothers, daughters, aunts, grandmothers, and granddaughters holding picket signs, singing hymns, clapping their hands. They knew that the March, like so many great moments, could not have happened without them.

Jackie Robinson, one of many celebrities at the March, with his family.

EVELYN CUNNINGHAM REMEMBERS

"I must've cried for an hour and half at one point during the March. Part of it was sheer happiness, part of it was pride, and part of it was my family. I'm steeped in my respect for my people. After the March, I thought, 'Oh my God, we're almost there . . . God, was I wrong.' "

I was covering the March for *The Pittsburgh Courier*. I can see this photograph of myself now from the press tent. I am standing near a phone, I'm reading my story into the New York office. I have my eyeglasses on my nose and I have a piece of paper in my hand.

I could see everything. I had a seat in the third row, reserved for the press. My third husband was with me in the audience. I had some kind of jive press credential that I gave to him. The only way I got to cover civil rights for the *Courier* was to cry, beg, scream, and do all of those things that female reporters did at the time. I went into the *Courier* with an attitude. I had dyed red hair and a mink coat. They thought I was expendable. But the guys on the city desk never challenged me. I knew how to deal with men. I had a father and brother who I adored. My first big story was when I was sent down South to cover the Autherine Lucy story. And then things started to happen in quick succession. Little Rock. Bull Connor. The killings...

I was in the thick of things. A. Philip Randolph always gave me quotes. I introduced him to Malcolm X. He knew that I knew Malcolm. Malcolm used to sit at the *Courier's* offices all the time. He and Randolph would talk about each other to me. One day Malcolm came by the office and was talking about the civil rights leadership, and he got on

Randolph, and I said, "Have you ever met him?" And he said, "No." Malcolm said, "A. Philip Randolph is the only one with any sense." I arranged a meeting of the two at a mosque at 117th and Lenox Avenue (in Harlem). Randolph came early. Malcolm sent someone to see if we were there. When he arrived, I left. I could just kick myself that I didn't stay to witness history being made. I never found out what the two of them talked about. I could've waited 'til they asked me to leave, you know?

Anna Arnold Hedgemen was one of the most unsung, unheralded people of the movement. I don't think she got the notice that she deserved. She did her homework. She had great courage and showed great leadership. She was soft spoken when she needed to be, but she could also raise her voice, and shake her finger. Daisy Bates was kind of fly. She was very attractive. She was sexy. She had a sense of her womanness. She was a wee bit of a flirt. Once they relaxed, it all came out. She'd get in touch with me. I liked her a lot. She had a lot of flair, but she was serious, and a hell of a leader...

Rustin was something else. He practically lived with Dr. Arthur Logan and his wife, Adele. They devoted a great deal of energy to the movement. They gave money, time, everything.

People were a little bit leery about whether the March on Washington would be a hit. But it was not a flop. Far from it. It was a giant hit. First off, the March melded so many different factions of black people like nothing else had ever done. We had so many different identities: There were the Ph.D. black folks, the shuffling Uncle Toms, the sports and entertainment folks. But there never appeared to be anything that focused on our commonality. The only time we all came together was if someone respectable was called a racial name. Never before was there anything that made us feel a sense of togetherness. The march made us realize that we were all in it together. The quality and the caliber of the people that it attracted…was…oh my. And the people who attended were saying that this was something that we must all do…act in common. For generations we'd been split. We'd say, "I can't join that group, because it's not my philosophy." We have to stop that. One of the reasons that I am an active, non-apologetic Republican is that if black people were sixty percent Democrat and forty percent Republican, we could get anything that we wanted…

No other speech compared to "I Have a Dream." But Randolph was a natural speaker. He was elegant. His manner was so impeccable. I liked all the white speakers. They were all out of their league. None had every done anything like this. They wanted to be there. They too had an awesome responsibility…

I must've cried for an hour and half at one point during the March. Part of it was sheer happiness, part of it was pride, and part of it was my family. I'm steeped in my respect for my people.

King never got all of this adulation when he was alive. I traveled a lot with him from town to town on the Hummingbird Express. I watched people's reactions. I had a nice, wonderful time with him. I got to worship and adore him. At the meetings and at the churches, at the beginning and end, when we sang "We Shall Overcome" to open and close the meetings, during the time, it was quite something…I still cry when we sing that song. He got respect in his day, but the respect was based on the fact that he was so young. I can still hear him say, "Sister Cunningham, I don't think you're really nonviolent."

After the March, I was drained. There was nothing that anyone could say to me. I couldn't speak myself. I don't care if the most famous person in the world came up to me, I wouldn't have said a word. I couldn't. It was one of those experiences that you just can't explain.

Dr. Martin Luther King, Jr. waves to the crowd after his " I Have a Dream" speech.

CHAPTER 8

AUGUST 28, 1963

The participants knew that if the March had changed no votes in Congress or no hearts in America that it had changed them... men and women would look back on this day and tell their children and their grandchildren: "There was a March in the middle of the twentieth century, the biggest demonstration for civil rights[in] history— and I was there."
—Lerone Bennett, Jr.

On the morning of the March on Washington for Jobs and Freedom, a brilliant red sun gently kissed the waters of the Reflecting Pool and rose high above a city that had not yet come fully alive. The city was shrouded in silence. No early birds singing, lawn mowers buzzing, cranky motors running. No noisy delivery trucks waiting to drop off bundles of the *Washington Post*. The city's well-scrubbed monuments were noticeably pristine on that last Wednesday in August. Its wide boulevards and lush green embankments were barren. The host city of the March on Washington resembled the setting of a 1960s science-fiction movie, where townspeople, fearing an attack of aliens, had deserted their beloved burg and left with all their belongings, down to their beaten-up coffee pots.

From their hotel rooms, the organizers of the March could watch the last dewdrops slowly drying up in the thirsty early morning sun. The days spent planning the March seemed to have evaporated just as quickly. Eight weeks—days and nights of planning, speaking, debating, reasoning, cajoling, compromising, writing, and editing—had come down to this moment. After making last-minute calls to several representatives on Capitol Hill, the organizers would take their seats on the dais, they hoped, before tens of thousands of people. Last-minute details more or less had been attended to by their deputies and their staffs. They had spoken to the bus captains the night before to finalize head counts. They said they were expecting thousands. Final telephone calls had been made, and telegrams had been sent. Invitations had been mailed. Now it was time to see the day through to the end.

As they knotted ties and straightened suits, it is conceivable that the organizers said prayers, silently and aloud, for thousands of people to join them on the day. The architects of the March would have to rely on supreme faith that tens of thousands of people would board buses, trains, cars, and planes and make their presence felt in the nation's capital.

By 6 A.M., there were whispers, but not from eager marchers. A flock of one hundred news reporters hovered together with their blank notebooks, holding pens, ready to tell viewers and readers about the multitude of marchers they expected from every corner of the country. For nearly ninety minutes, they waited for a train to arrive, as a few early birds began to assemble near the Washington Monument. In fact, as Nan Robertson reported in *The New York Times*, "there were probably more cops than marchers on the assembly grounds around the Washington Monument." Together they made a formidable force—"club-carrying firemen, national guards, police reserves, soldiers and marines," with helicopters ready to swoop down, if necessary.

As the reporters and police officers exchanged anecdotes, theories about how this would unfold, rumors of arrests, and celebrity sightings, something happened:

At 7:25 A.M., the first train from Baltimore arrived in Union Station. Spilling out of its doors were a horde of folks—black and white, arm in arm, hand in hand, carrying paper bags and placards, laughing and talking. They were a sight to behold: black, brown, and beige; white, tan, and bronze; every shade of black imaginable, hands interlocked. As they walked, they raised their voices in a mighty choir.

They came to the city in tiny clusters: families, church and school groups. They walked with refinement, elegance, and poise. Group by group, this "gentle army" made its descent upon the city. Strangers talked like neighbors; neighbors talked like family. As they made their way to the assembly grounds to check in, they "brushed past Sammy Davis, Jr. and Diahann Carroll," according to the *Richmond Afro American*, with awe but very determined to get to the proceedings. It was clear that in this gathering, fame faded into the background. This day, real people from real places were dealing with real democratic issues.

Between 8 A.M. and noon, 21 special trains and 16 regular trains unloaded their passengers into Union Station. Nearly 4,000 passengers arrived on one from Chicago. Soon, folks from Newark, Philadelphia, and Baltimore arrived—25,000 strong. They entered the city, alert and armed with enthusiasm. Someone from Philadelphia said there would be 32,000 coming from the City of Brotherly Love. Folks from Cleveland and Columbus, Denver and Detroit, Indianapolis and Minneapolis emerged from buses and trains. A freedom train from Jacksonville, Florida that had swept through the South released an energetic group who burst into applause.

Together and separately, in harmony and off-key, they sang familiar freedom songs: "Ain't Gon' Let Nobody Turn Me Round" and "Oh Freedom." They had sung these songs in their houses of worship, and in their parlor rooms. They had marched on dirt roads in the South and broken concrete in the North, but the fractured choirs became one. Young and old, man and woman, black and white were one mighty force walking, switching, striding, gliding, shoulder to shoulder, side by side. They walked up Constitution Avenue, and alongside the March's headquarters. There was a huge green-and-white tent that reporters said looked like a circus tent, but folks in the most rural parts of the Delta, the swamps of Florida, the sand hills of the Carolinas, the flatlands of Texas, and the concrete of Northeastern and Midwestern cities knew, this was a revival tent. And their spirits would be revived. They were prepared to listen, respond, and rejoice.

Some threw their hands jubilantly into the air. Others placed their hands on their hearts. Parents mouthed the words with their children. Some burst into tears. Meanwhile, the March leaders busied themselves with several meetings on Capitol Hill with various elected officials.

With thousands spilling onto the monument grounds at 9:30 A.M., the playwright and actor Ossie Davis announced the start of the midmorning entertainment. The performances were varied—folk songs and poetry readings mixed with spirituals. Joan Baez opened with a heartfelt rendition of the anthems "Oh Freedom," and "We Shall Overcome." Beatniks joined hands with members of the northern black elite; sharecroppers clapped hands with Midwestern socialites. The actress Ruby Dee stilled the crowd with an elegant reading of Margaret Walker's poem "For My People." The folk singer Odetta stirred the crowd with ringing versions of "O' Freedom Over Me" and "I'm on My Way." Carried away in the moment, Josh White, Baez, and Mary of the Peter, Paul and Mary trio joined Odetta in song. Bob Dylan sang a tribute to Medgar Evers, and invited the SNCC singers to share their amazing voices with the crowd. Shortly after Odetta sang, Roy Wilkins announced that W.E.B. DuBois had died in his sleep in Ghana.

Some of the crowd began to grow restless. People seemed eager to start walking. For a moment, there was a sense of organized chaos evident only through the loudspeakers, as captured by *The New York Times*:

"WE ARE TRYING TO LOCATE MISS LENA HORNE…"

Simultaneously, a smattering of church groups began to hold hands and bow their heads in prayer. "Lord, Jesus, we thank you…"

"LENA—WHEREVER YOU ARE—"

Before the glamorous Miss Horne could work the crowd into a frenzy, some groups walked away from the monument grounds, transforming Constitution and Independence Avenues "into oceans of bobbing placards: Some marchers wept as they walked; the faces of many more beamed with happiness. There were no brass bands. There was little shouting or singing. Instead, for over an hour and a half, there was the sound of thousands of marching feet toward the temple erected in the name of Abraham Lincoln."

Back at the Monument Grounds, the loudspeaker continued: "BOBBY DARIN."

The pop singer, obviously moved, attempted to sing. "Here as a singer and I'm proud and I'm kind of choked up." After Darin's performance, spontaneously, and without advice from the platform, the remaining crowds flowed away, moving en masse toward the Lincoln Memorial.

Shortly before noon, the crowd collected at the Lincoln Memorial, where the speakers' platform was set on the top step.

Newsweek described the moment perfectly: "Under the brooding marble gaze of Abraham Lincoln, their leaders watched the tributary streams—mothers and daughters, fathers and sons—spill down along the avenues and the grassy banks of the Reflecting Pool, eddying into the pointillist seascape of faces below them."

At the Lincoln Memorial, Josephine Baker, who fled St. Louis during the Jazz Age and became an international sensation based in Paris, made a surprise appearance at the March. She'd flown in from the City of Light.

"You are on the eve of a complete victory," she said as she made her way through the crowd. "You can't go wrong. The world is behind you."

The crowd now measured in the tens of thousands. Many were simply enjoying the day, having brought picnic baskets and thermos jugs and camp stools. They "lunched leisurely in the soft August sunshine. Some stretched out to doze on the grass."

The famous—Charlton Heston, Burt Lancaster, Paul Newman, Joanne Woodward, Anthony Franciosa, Rita Moreno, Susan Strasberg, Dennis Hopper, James Garner, Sidney Poitier, Harry Belafonte, and

Marlon Brando—blended in with a sea of everyday people.

As the sun bore its might down on the crowd, marchers gathered around the Reflecting Pool and began to cool their heels in its warm water. Some began to fan themselves with their programs. The heat didn't faze others, who were caught up in the spirit of the moment, according to *Newsweek:*

"All the beautiful women here want—FREEDOM! All the handsome men here want—FREEDOM!"

From the tents, the organizers watched the growing flock in amazement. Before their eyes were more than 200,000 people—from every walk of life—to support the cause. They were witnessing more than a crowd of marching, clapping, singing, shouting people; they were watching history, surprising and surreal, unfold before their eyes.

When a *New York Times* reporter asked the writer James Baldwin to explain how he felt, he answered, "I'd have to cry. Or sing."

By 1 P.M., the steps outside the monument filled with so many people that the speakers' stand was partially hidden from view. Still, there was a courtesy and order that emanated throughout the crowd.

"Excuse me…"

"I'm so sorry, I didn't mean to step on your foot."

"Pardon me. Goodness, do I know you?"

As the program began, the hordes of marchers squeezed in to see Marian Anderson, who was to lead the National Anthem. However, Anderson was caught in the crowd, trying to make her way to the stage. The *Richmond Afro American* reported that "Camilla Williams, a talented soprano whose Danville, Virginia hometown had been torn with racial strife, launched the ceremonies at the Memorial with a moving rendition of the Anthem. Later, Anderson provided a stirring rendition of 'He's Got the Whole World in His Hands.'"

The crowd applauded wildly for Miss Williams. If there was any tension, it was beyond the crowd and within the ranks of the organizers. Rustin was frantic, pacing back and forth. Elated on one hand, exhausted on another, he had the people. His and Randolph's dream had come true. Now he had to make it mean something. To be sure, it was meaningful that 200,000 people came to Washington to demand a full exercise of democracy, but it had to be memorable as a political event as well. In addition to the brouhaha over John Lewis's speech, Rustin was trying to soothe both Baldwin and Fred Shuttlesworth, whose names had been omitted from the program.

In the middle of this contretemps, the Most Rev. Patrick O'Boyle, Archbishop of Washington, offered the invocation: "In the name of the Father and of the Son and of the Holy Ghost, amen…Bless this nation and all its people. May the warmth of Your love replace the coldness that springs from prejudice and bitterness. Send in our midst the Holy Spirit to open the eyes of all to the great truth that all men are equal in Your Sight. Let us understand that simple justice demands that the rights of all be honored by every man…"

The sight of more than two hundred thousand bowed heads in prayer, hands reaching to the heavens, had to be an emotional moment for A. Philip Randolph, who took the stage to offer the opening remarks. Twenty-two years later, his dream had come true. The tall, distinguished gentleman leaned into the microphone, and spoke:

Fellow Americans, we are gathered here in the largest demonstration in the history of this nation. Let the nation and the world know the meaning of our numbers. We are not a pressure group, we are not an organization or a group of organizations, we are not a mob. We are the advance guard of a massive moral revolution for jobs and freedom. This revolution reverberates throughout the land touching every city, every town, every village where black men are segregated, oppressed, and exploited.

But this Civil Rights Movement is not confined to the Negroes; nor is it confined to civil rights. Our white allies know that they cannot be free while we are not. And we know that we have no interest in a society in which six million black and white people are unemployed, and millions more live in poverty . . . We here, today, are only the first wave. When we leave, it will be to carry on the civil rights revolution home

125

*with us, into every nook and cranny of the land. And we shall return
again and again to Washington in ever growing numbers until total freedom is ours.*

The crowd burst into applause, especially those marchers who
recalled Randolph's trips throughout the country to rally support for
the first March on Washington. Some wiped tears with the back of
their hands as they clapped.

Before Randolph could introduce the next speaker, Rustin shoved
Shuttlesworth onto the stage for impromptu banter. The crowd nod-
ded knowingly and with reverence when the Rev. Eugene Carson
Blake of the National Council of Churches addressed them: "For
many years now the National Council of Churches and most of its
constituent members have said all the right things about civil rights.
Out official pronouncements for years have clearly called for a 'nonsegregated church in a nonsegregated society.' But as of August 28,
1963, we have achieved neither a nonsegregated church nor a nonsegregated society. And it is partially because the churches of America
have failed to put their own houses in order that 100 years after the
Emancipation Proclamation, 175 years after the adoption of the
Constitution, 173 years after the adoption of the Bill of Rights, the
United States of America still faces a racial crisis."

According to Thomas Gentile in *The March on Washington*, "Dr.
Blake recognized that he and his fellow churchmen shared the blame
for the plight of American Negroes [since] churches had failed to put
their own houses in order."

Next up was the "Tribute to Negro Women Freedom Fighters."
Daisy Bates, the Arkansas NAACP director and fearless leader of the
Little Rock Central High School desegregation in 1957, filled in for
Myrlie Evers, who was speaking in Boston. When Evers' name was
announced, the crowd erupted into loud applause.

Diane Nash Bevel, Rosa Parks, Gloria Richardson and Mrs.
Herbert Lee were on the platform. Daisy Bates spoke for all of them

when she said: "The women of this country, Mr. Randolph, pledge to you, to Martin Luther King, Roy Wilkins and all of you fighting for civil liberties, that we will join hands with you as women of this country. We will kneel-in, we will sit-in, until we can eat in any counter in the United States. We will walk until we are free, until we can walk to any school and take our children to any school in the United States. And we will sit-in and we will kneel-in and we will line-in if necessary until every Negro in America can vote. This we pledge you. The women of America."

Bates' words echoed through a polite, reverent crowd. (There was not even a hint of the violence officials had feared would erupt.)

Afterward, Bob Dylan performed the song "Only a Pawn in Their Game," followed by Odetta, Joan Baez, and Peter, Paul and Mary.

Next up was John Lewis, chairman of the Student Nonviolent Coordinating Committee. Although Lewis had toned down his speech, he still electrified the crowd:

"My friends," he said, "let us not forget that we are involved in a serious revolution. But by and large American politics is dominated by politicians who build their career on immoral compromising and ally themselves with open forums of political, economic, and social exploitation." He concluded: "They're talking about slow down and stop. We will not stop. If we do not get meaningful legislation out of this Congress, the time will come when we will not confine our marching to Washington. We will march through the South, through the streets of Danville, through the streets of Cambridge, through the streets of Birmingham. But we will march with the spirit of love and the spirit of dignity that we have shown here today."

(In the original text, Lewis had written: "We will not wait for the President, the Justice Department, nor the Congress, but we will take matters into our own hands and create a source of power, outside of any national structure, that could and would assure us a victory." He had also written: "We will march through the heart of Dixie, the way Sherman did.")

If labor leader Walter Reuther had not followed Lewis—whom the crowd would've cheered until dawn—Reuther would have received even more thunderous applause. The crowd cheered loudly when he told them: "I am here today with you because with you I share the view that the struggle for equal opportunity is not the struggle for Negro Americans, but the struggle for every American to join in. For one hundred years the Negro people have searched for first class citizenship, and I believe that they cannot and should not wait until some distant tomorrow. They should demand freedom now! Here and now! It is the responsibility of every American to share the impatience of the Negro Americans."

Indeed, as Gay Talese reported in *The New York Times*, a small crowd watching television at the Barber Queen, a shop on 125th Street in Harlem, said, " That Reuther made a helluva speech, didn't he? "

The speeches were also cheered by millions watching their black-and-white television sets. The March, according to Steven Kasher in *The Civil Rights Movement: A Photographic History, 1954-68,* "was one of the first events to be broadcast live around the world, via the newly launched communications satellite Telstar. The three major networks spent more than three hundred thousand dollars to broadcast the event. CBS covered the March from 1:30 to 4:30 P.M., pre-empting *As the World Turns, Password, Art Linkletter's House Party, To Tell the Truth, The Edge of Night* and *Secret Storm.*"

As time passed, the crowd grew even larger. It was as if the flow of people would never stop. The intense sun wearied the crowd, and interest began to wane. There were random conversations, and some whispering, but it didn't last for long. The marchers began to realize the magnitude of the event, and without explanation there was a breakout of tears and random cries of joy. And even more tears came when the message of James Farmer, the CORE leader, who was in a Louisiana jail, was delivered by Floyd B. McKissick:

"From a South Louisiana parish jail, I salute the March on Washington for Jobs and Freedom...We will not slow down; we will not stop our militant, peaceful demonstrations; we will not come off of the streets until we can work at a job befitting our skills...we will not stop our marching people until our kids have enough to eat and their minds can study a wide range without being cramped in Jim Crow schools."

Next to speak was the Rabbi Uri Miller, president of the Synagogue Council of America. In his eloquent talk, he asked those present to "understand that he who discriminates is as morally hurt as is the one discriminated against, physically hurt."

Sometime between Miller's talk and Whitney Young's, the heat became unbearable. Journalists present reported that "people grew weak and fainted and were passed from hand to hand over the fence to first aides, who laid them gently on the ground."

Despite the heat, Whitney Young did his part, shoring up the troops to take action once they left the capital:

"This march must go beyond this historic moment," said Young. "For the true test of the rededication and the commitment, which should flow from this meeting, will be in our recognition that, however incensed our Congressional representatives are by this demonstration, they will not act because of it alone. We must support the strong, we must give courage to the timid, we must remind the indifferent, and warn the opposed: Civil rights, which are God-given and constitutionally guaranteed, are not negotiable in 1963."

After Mathew Ahmann of the Catholic Conference for Interracial Justice spoke, Randolph introduced Wilkins as "the acknowledged leader of the Civil Rights Movement in America."

Instead of beginning his prepared address straightaway, Wilkins opened by saying that he was the bearer of news of solemn and great significance, Dr. W.E.B. DuBois was dead in Ghana, the country of his adopted citizenship.

Wilkins, who reminded some of "a proper Protestant pastor or one of the older men behind the counter at Brooks Brothers," praised both DuBois' contribution to the movement, and his fiery independence:

"Regardless of the fact that in his later years, Dr. DuBois chose another path," Wilkins told the suddenly still crowd, "it is incontrovertible that at the dawn of the twentieth century his was the voice calling you to gather here today in this cause." Wilkins requested a moment of silence, and a sense of "poignancy" overcame the marchers. Wilkins' tone was less fiery than Lewis', but his words were hard-hitting nonetheless. He made it plain that he and his colleagues thought the President's civil rights bill did not go nearly far enough:

We came here to speak to our Congress, to those men and women who speak here for us in that marble forum over yonder on the hill.

Now, my friends, all over this land, and especially in the Deep South. We are beaten and kicked and maltreated and shot and killed by local and state law enforcement. It is simply incomprehensible to us here today and to millions of others far from this spot that the United States government, which can regulate the contents of a pill, apparently is powerless to prevent the physical abuse of citizens within its own borders.

The president's proposals represent so moderate an approach that if any one is weakened or eliminated, the remainder will be little more than sugar water. Indeed, the package needs strengthening…

Wilkins closed with this admonition: "Remember Luke's account of the warning to us all: 'No man, having put his hand to the plow, and looking back, is fit for the Kingdom of God.'"

The *Richmond Afro American* reported that "there were hundreds who could not restrain their tears when Mahalia Jackson sang, 'Lord, Stand by Me,' and 'I've Been 'Buked and I've Been Scorned,' and climaxed the moment with hands on her hips and arms raised" heavenward. Jackson's musical tribute was an emotional high point for the crowd. "The button-down men in front and the old women in back came to their feet screaming and shouting. They had not known that this thing was in them, and that they wanted it touched." If Jackson touched the crowd, Dr. King would move them into places that, spiritually and emotionally, they had never known.

King was preceded on the podium by Rabbi Joachim Prinz, president of the American Jewish Congress, whose words were a reminder of the urgency of confronting any challenge to democracy:

"When I was the rabbi of the Jewish community in Berlin under the Hitler regime, I learned many things. The most important thing that I learned in my life and under those tragic circumstances is that bigotry and hatred are not the most urgent problem. The most urgent, the most shameful and the most tragic problem is silence..."

"A great people which had created a great civilization had become a nation of silent onlookers. They remained silent in the face of hate, in the face of brutality and in the face of mass murder. America must not become a nation of onlookers. America must not remain silent. Not merely black America, but all of America..."

Randolph stood to introduce King, calling him "the moral leader of our nation," and applause followed for nearly a minute. Disciples and followers of Dr. King had heard variations of his "I Have a Dream" speech. In fact, according to John Lewis, "he had recited the essence of the speech" in Detroit "a week earlier." But as Lewis acknowledged, "this was a different audience, a different time, a different place. This was truly history, and Dr. King knew it. We all knew it."

And so Dr. King spoke:

Five score years ago, a great American, in whose symbolic shadow we stand today, signed the Emancipation Proclamation. This momentous decree came as a great beacon light of hope to millions of Negro slaves who had been seared in the flames of withering injustice. It came as a joyous daybreak to end the long night of their captivity. But one hundred years later, we must face the tragic fact that the Negro is still not free.

One hundred years later, the life of the Negro is still sadly crippled by the manacles of segregation and the chains of discrimination. One hundred years later, the Negro lives on a lonely island of poverty in the midst of a vast ocean of material prosperity. One hundred years later, the

Negro is still languishing in the corners of American society and finds himself an exile in his own land.

So we have come here today to dramatize an appalling condition. In a sense we have come to our nation's capital to cash a check. When the architects of our republic wrote the magnificent words of the Constitution and the Declaration of Independence, they were signing a promissory note to which every American was to fall heir.

This note was a promise that all men would be guaranteed the inalienable rights of life, liberty, and the pursuit of happiness. It is obvious today that America has defaulted on this promissory note insofar as her citizens of color are concerned. Instead of honoring this sacred obligation, America has given the Negro people a bad check, which has come back marked "insufficient funds." But we refuse to believe that the bank of justice is bankrupt. We refuse to believe that there are insufficient funds in the great vaults of opportunity of this nation.

So we have come to cash this check — a check that will give us upon demand the riches of freedom and the security of justice. We have also come to this hallowed spot to remind America of the fierce urgency of now. This is no time to engage in the luxury of cooling off or to take the tranquilizing drug of gradualism. Now is the time to rise from the dark and desolate valley of segregation to the sunlit path of racial justice.

Now is the time to open the doors of opportunity to all of God's children. Now is the time to lift our nation from the quicksands of racial injustice to the solid rock of brotherhood.

It would be fatal for the nation to overlook the urgency of the moment and to underestimate the determination of the Negro. This sweltering summer of the Negro's legitimate discontent will not pass until there is an invigorating autumn of freedom and equality. Nineteen sixty-three is not an end, but a beginning. Those who hope that the Negro needed to blow off steam and will now be content will have a rude awakening if the nation returns to business as usual. There will be neither rest nor tranquility in America until the Negro is granted his citizenship rights.

The whirlwinds of revolt will continue to shake the foundations of our nation until the bright day of justice emerges. But there is something that I must say to my people who stand on the warm threshold that leads into the palace of justice. In the process of gaining our rightful place we must not be guilty of wrongful deeds. Let us not seek to satisfy our thirst for freedom by drinking from the cup of bitterness and hatred.

We must forever conduct our struggle on the high plane of dignity and discipline. We must not allow our creative protest to degenerate into physical violence. Again and again we must rise to the majestic heights of meeting physical force with soul force.

The marvelous new militancy which has engulfed the Negro community must not lead us to distrust of all white people, for many of our white brothers, as evidenced by their presence here today, have come to realize that their destiny is tied up with our destiny and their freedom is inextricably bound to our freedom.

We cannot walk alone. And as we walk, we must make the pledge that we shall march ahead. We cannot turn back. There are those who are asking the devotees of civil rights, "When will you be satisfied?" We can never be satisfied as long as our bodies, heavy with the fatigue of travel, cannot gain lodging in the motels of the highways and the hotels of the cities. We cannot be satisfied as long as the Negro's basic mobility is from a smaller ghetto to a larger one. We can never be satisfied as long as a Negro in Mississippi cannot vote and a Negro in New York believes he has nothing for which to vote. No, no, we are not satisfied, and we will not be satisfied until justice rolls down like waters and righteousness like a mighty stream.

I am not unmindful that some of you have come here out of great trials and tribulations. Some of you have come fresh from narrow cells. Some of you have come from areas where your quest for freedom left you battered by the storms of persecution and staggered by the winds of police brutality. You have been the veterans of creative suffering. Continue to work with the faith that unearned suffering is redemptive.

Go back to Mississippi, go back to Alabama, go back to Georgia, go back to Louisiana, go back to the slums and ghettos of our Northern cities, knowing that somehow this situation can and will be changed. Let us not wallow in the valley of despair. At the moment, I still have a dream. It is a dream deeply rooted in the American dream.

I have a dream that one day this nation will rise up and live out the true meaning of its creed: "We hold these truths to be self-evident: that all men are created equal." I have a dream that one day on the red hills of Georgia the sons of former slaves and the sons of former slave owners will be able to sit down together at a table of brotherhood. I have a dream that one day even the state of Mississippi, a desert state, sweltering with the heat of injustice and oppression, will be transformed into an oasis of freedom and justice. I have a dream that my four children will one day live in a nation where they will not be judged by the color of their skin but by the content of their character. I have a dream today.

I have a dream that one day the state of Alabama, whose governor's lips are presently dripping with the words of interposition and nullification, will be transformed into a situation where little black boys and black girls will be able to join hands with little white boys and white girls and walk together as sisters and brothers. I have a dream today. I have a dream that one day every valley shall be exalted, every hill and mountain shall be made low, the rough places will be made plain, and the crooked places will be made straight, and the glory of the Lord shall be revealed, and all flesh shall see it together.

This is our hope. This is the faith with which I return to the South. With this faith we will be able to hew out of the mountain of despair a stone of hope. With this faith we will be able to transform the jangling discords of our nation into a beautiful symphony of brotherhood. With this faith we will be able to work together, to pray together, to struggle together, to go to jail together, to stand up for freedom together, knowing that we will be free one day.

This will be the day when all of God's children will be able to sing with a new meaning, "My country, 'tis of thee, sweet land of liberty, of thee I sing. Land where my fathers died, land of the pilgrim's pride, from every mountainside, let freedom ring." And if America is to be a great nation, this must become true. So let freedom ring from the prodigious hilltops of New Hampshire. Let freedom ring from the mighty mountains of New York. Let freedom ring from the heightening Alleghenies of Pennsylvania! Let freedom ring from the snowcapped Rockies of Colorado! Let freedom ring from the curvaceous peaks of California! But not only that; let freedom ring from Stone Mountain of Georgia! Let freedom ring from Lookout Mountain of Tennessee! Let freedom ring from every hill and every molehill of Mississippi. From every mountainside, let freedom ring.

When we let freedom ring, when we let it ring from every village and every hamlet, from every state and every city, we will be able to speed up that day when all of God's children, black men and white men, Jews and Gentiles, Protestants and Catholics, will be able to join hands and sing in the words of the old Negro spiritual, "Free at last! Free at last! Thank God Almighty, we are free at last!"

There was nothing more for King to say. When he finished, the crowd screamed, cheered, cried. Then they sat down quietly, wondering at the thing that had happened to them. From inside the White House, President Kennedy watched in awe: "He's damn good," he said to his aides.

Response to the speech was immediate. James Reston wrote in *The New York Times*: "It was Dr. King, who, near the end of the day, touched the vast audience. Until then the pilgrimage was merely a great spectacle." But Lerone Bennett, Jr. best summarized the response to the speech in *Ebony*:

It was not so much the words, eloquent as they were, as the manner of their saying: the rhythms and the intonations and the halts and breaks. These called back all the old men and women who had had this dream and had died dishonored; called back rickety Negro churches on dirt roads and the men and women who sat in them, called them back and found them not wanting, nor their hoping in vain. The rhythms and the intonation called back all the struggle and all the pain and all the agony, and held forth the possibility of triumph; they called back Emmett Till and Medgar Evers and all the others; called back ropes and chains and bombs and screams in the night; called back one-room walk-up flats . . . called them back and said they would soon be over.

Although the March program was running a half-hour ahead of schedule, Rustin wanted nothing to slow the momentum. Rustin led the crowd in the 10 Demands of the March. After each demand, Rustin asked, "What do you say?" They responded with a roaring echo.

"The demands included passage of the Civil Rights Bill without compromise or filibuster, withholding of federal funds from discriminatory programs, a ban on discrimination in housing, retraining programs to combat unemployment due to automation, an increased minimum wage, immediate school desegregation, and a Fair Employment Practices Act," according to Thomas Gentile in *The March on Washington*.

Randolph led the crowd in a pledge:

Standing before the Lincoln Memorial on the 28th of August, in the centennial year of emancipation, I affirm my complete personal commitment for the struggle for jobs and freedom for all Americans.

To fulfill that commitment, I pledge that I will not relax until victory is won.

I pledge that I will join and support all actions undertaken in good faith in accord with time-honored democratic traditions of nonviolent protest, or peaceful assembly and petition, and of redress through the courts and the legislative process.

I pledge to carry the message of the March to my friends and neighbors back home and to arouse them to an equal commitment and an equal effort. I will march and I will write letters. I will demonstrate and I will vote. I will work and make sure that my voice and those of my brothers ring clear and determined from every corner of our land.

I will pledge my heart and my mind and my body, unequivocally and without regard to personal sacrifice, to the achievement of social peace through social justice.

At 4:15 P.M., Dr. Benjamin E. Mays of Morehouse College delivered the benediction. The program ended with everyone singing "We Shall Overcome."

According to Kasher, "as the crowd withdrew, Rustin noticed

Randolph standing alone at the dais. He walked over and put his arm around the old man's shoulder and said, 'Mr. Randolph, it looks like your dream has come true.' Randolph replied that it was 'the most beautiful and glorious day of my life.' Tears flowed down his face."

There were no major incidents, no riots or disruptions, with the exception of American Nazi Party leader George Lincoln Rockwell, who, "prohibited by cops from crossing over to the Monument Grounds," raged helplessly:

"I can't stand niggers. I can't stand to hear "We Shall Overcome."

Immediately after the March, the President invited the leaders to the White House for "tea and sympathy and blunt political advice." For more than an hour he reiterated that "very strong bipartisan support" would be needed to get civil rights legislation enacted this year. The leaders listened. According to writer James Reston, some argued with Kennedy, but everyone knew, including Kennedy, that what they had just experienced "combined a number of things no politician could ignore: it had the force of numbers. And it was able to invoke the principles of the Founding Fathers, to rebuke the inequalities and hypocrisies of modern American life."

The marchers, exhausted and exhilarated, headed home, as crew members picked up the remnants of one of the greatest moments in American history.

By sundown, the city was silent, yet again.

James Baldwin: "I'd have to cry. Or sing."

VERTAMAE GROSVENOR REMEMBERS

"There was a real feeling of excitement mixed with anxiety in the air. There was the feeling that anything could happen to you at any time. No one was safe from an insult or worse. It was like, 'Oh God, they got Medgar,' 'Oh God, they got Malcolm,' so everyone was just holding their breath, not knowing what was going to happen, but we just kept moving on, you know?"

Were you at the March on Washington? That's all everyone asked after it happened. I would reply, "Yes, I was. I didn't see you there." The March on Washington was a great source of pride for us because it was such a huge success. I was reminded of that whole period recently when I saw this man at the grocery store. I can tell he was still attached to the 60s because of the way he was dressed. He approached me and said, "Congress of African People. Philadelphia." I answered, "yes." And I remembered that I used to go to everything during the time.

There was this great mixture of politics and poetry. People would turn out for a poetry reading like it was a rock concert. On the cultural side, there was a real rallying call to get people to come out. There was a real feeling of excitement mixed with anxiety in the air. There was the feeling that anything could happen to you at any time. No one was safe from an insult or worse. It was like, 'Oh God, they got Medgar.' 'Oh God, they got Malcolm,' so everyone was just holding their breath, not knowing what was going to happen, but we just kept moving on, you know?

There had always been an odd freedom in New York, if you aligned yourself with identifying yourself as being in the struggle. A lot of people don't talk about the divisions. A lot of people weren't ready for the changes that were to come. You would have poor people say, "Ain't nobody going to make me wear my hair natural." And within that statement, there were issues that we were ignoring, because the sense of something bigger—the murder of men, women, children, black, white—was out there. I wore headwraps, wigs, and afros. It was rough dealing with white and black people.

I remember when the four girls died in Birmingham. After the girls died, there was a movement to wear black arm bands in their memory. I took my daughters to a neighbor's house on the Upper West Side. When we walked into the party with the arm bands on, people were very uncomfortable. You could read their minds through their faces. It was a feeling of, "Why would you spoil the party with something like that?" One of the children asked my daughter, why do you have that on your arm? And she said, "It's for Addie Mae Collins."

The feeling among the adults was one of my introducing controversy to the children. I'll never forget how they reacted to this memory, and it was something like a few weeks after the March on Washington.

Today, things have changed. There are things that are so much better. How do we have to change to go along with the change? This is a totally different world for us, our children and our grandchildren. Where do "they" think that we can fit in? The "they" these days are a small group of people, who don't think in color. They are going on plotting the world. It's naïve to think that white people are just trying to keep black people out of things. And some things haven't changed at all. Sometimes, whether it's real or imagined, if we think an incident has to do with color, others think it has nothing to do with color, and they say people were just having a bad day. See me on one of my bad days.

There's a great deal of indifference. It's not like before where we used to see black people and there was a bond. I went to an affair and there were about 75 people, and there was one black man who went out of his way to avoid me. It was like, God forbid if white people should see us talking.

During that period, we were trying to bond. It was like we were one family. There was a lot of "my sister, my brother"' We'd move from Negro to black. Today, when you say black, people think urban or hip-hop. If you say, "my daughter's dating the most wonderful young black man," and they think, she's going out with somebody with their pants hanging down.

NAN GROGAN ORROCK REMEMBERS

"I realized the depths of the degradation of segregation; the complete unacceptability of being a second-class citizen. To know that I was in the presence of such courage—people were losing jobs, homes, and physically placing their lives on the line—was a life-altering experience for me."

In 1963, I was a student at Mary Washington College. I wasn't involved in politics, nor was I sensitized on race. There hadn't been any local manifestations of the struggle in Staunton, Virginia, where I lived. During the summer, I stayed with my aunt, who lived on [Capitol] Hill. I worked in an integrated office, which was an enlightening experience. I had begun to develop friendships with my office mates. The March had been in the news throughout the summer. There was a big rumble in the district that there was this huge unknown, threatening phenomenon approaching. There were wide reports about how people weren't coming to work. It was as if the city was under siege. There were accounts of people sitting on their front porches with guns.

I decided to go on the basis of people in the office. I was clearly not hostile to civil rights, but I never had any focus on the issue either. I didn't tell my aunt what I was doing. The morning of the March a white co-worker—the first white liberal I had ever met—picked me up a ways from my aunt's apartment.

You couldn't help but get swept up in the feeling of the March. It was an incredible experience of this mass of humanity with one mind moving down the street. It was like being a part of a glacier. You could feel the sense of collective will and effort in the air. I was in awe at the number of people. And I was struck by a group carrying a banner from

Danville, Virginia, which had been the site of some very bad beatings. I talked with the people from Danville, which was not far from Staunton. I was overwhelmed by their bravery; how they'd held on to their ideals. They'd placed themselves in harm's way. They could be killed. That encounter gave me an insight that I hadn't had. I realized the depths of the degradation of segregation; the complete unacceptability of being a second-class citizen. To know that I was in the presence of such courage—people were losing jobs, homes, and physically placing their lives on the line—was a life altering experience for me.

All at once, I learned several valuable lessons from that encounter and that day. The first was how blind I was to these realities. Seeing and talking to different people at the March pulled my blinders off. I was struck by how incredibly sheltered and shielded I was from an entire population. By virtue of my being white, I didn't have to be a victim of oppression. I was struck by the privilege that I had. I thought I knew a lot about the world, and here was this enormous reality in front of me, and I had the luxury of being oblivious. And yet I thought of myself as learned, educated, and well-read.

Another experience was the solidarity, power, and strength that can be achieved in collective action. I thought, "This is huge. This can change things. This is making a statement that cannot be ignored." I believed that this is a manifestation...this was empowering. Now, we didn't use those words back then, but I knew that this march was the manifestation of a movement that wasn't going to be turned back..."

Once I got to the Mall and the Reflecting Pool, I saw this mass of humanity—people from all of these different towns, especially from the South.

You couldn't see far enough. Hearing Dr. King speak was

a very powerful experience. I wasn't coming to this experience with a solid feeling for all that had come before. All of this was an experience that I hadn't thought about to any degree. The leap that I made, how sharply the situation came into focus, it put me in an entirely new place.

I was so caught up in the day that I hadn't stopped to think about all of the television cameras. And when I realized that the March was being filmed, I panicked. I thought, "I'm going to be seen on television, and the cat will be out of the bag, and my family will see me." I was 20 and I still hadn't cut the apron strings.

I didn't tell my relatives where I had been. Within a month or two, I told someone and they told everyone, so the word got out. My idea that I had to hide my going to the March was confirmed. When I returned to school, I joined the Race Relations Committee. The YWCA was the only place to find people who wanted to talk about race. Mary Washington College was a segregated school until 1965, when they admitted the first black student. I sit on the board of the YWCA in Atlanta because of what they did to help bridge the racial divide when I was in school. In the spring of 1964, the YWCA brought women to Atlanta. We were trained in voter registration. I met Dr. King. I met SNCC people my age. We did house to house voter registration in the old buttermilk bottle district. I came back that summer to work with SNCC. The one experience with the people of Danville at the March was pivotal. I organized my life and activities and decisions to change the fundamental reality of democracy. I began to understand the women's movement, miltarism, and labor issues.

I never lost an appreciation for mass action and its ability to create change. I saw it happen to me. The power of that experience was singular. And it's something that's stayed with me: people getting out and moving together. You can get out of touch with the reality. It remains true forty years later. Stepping forward can move you into another area of consciousness. When people stand up and make up their minds to move and take action, it opens doors and moves them to new places.

EPILOGUE

The March on Washington far exceeded the expectations of its organizers. The sight of more than 250,000 Americans gathered in the nation's capital to protest inequality in the United States captured the world's attention. The March touched the world's people—emotionally, spiritually, and politically—in ways they had never been touched before. The three networks—ABC, CBS, and NBC—beamed coverage throughout the world. As *The New York Times* noted, "uncounted millions from Accra to Zanzibar turned their eyes to Washington as they have for few other events in American history." They saw the faces— black and white, young and old, powerful and poor, and they saw the people standing, marching, applauding, pleading for equality in the land where it was supposed to be a birthright. No matter the language or translation, viewers in Amsterdam, Athens, Buenos Aires, Cairo, London, Paris, Berlin, Rome, Tel Aviv, Tokyo, and other cities around the world were awakened by the cheers and tears, silent prayers and thundering applause of a diverse gathering of Americans crying for freedom—the sound heard all around the world. Its echo lingered long after the marchers departed Washington, D.C.

While viewers and listeners focused on the message of freedom that emanated from the March, the mainstream press in the United States focused on the "quiet, dignified manner" of the crowd, and how "well-behaved" and "peaceful" they were while they were in Washington for the day. Certainly anyone who had followed the news coverage could see that these civil rights activists were not angry, loud, or violent. It was the bloodshed against these activists in parts of Mississippi, Alabama and Georgia that first gained the world's attention. Long after the March was over, the attendees would go home, and live with the memory of an extraordinary day, but also the pain of lost leaders, mourning mothers, murdered young men and women, and frightened children. The pain and terror that ran throughout black communities, especially throughout the South, was real. The despair and disappointment in blighted, overcrowded Northern and Midwestern cities was real.

"In the days that followed," said John Lewis, "too much of the national press, in my opinion, focused not on the substance of the day, but on the setting. Their stories portrayed the event as a big picnic, a hootenanny combined with the spirit of a revival prayer meeting. Too many commentators and reporters softened and trivialized the hard edges of pain and suffering that brought about this day in the first place, virtually ignoring the hard issues that needed to be addressed."

Indeed, there was an exuberance that rang throughout the March. It was a success because so few people thought that it would happen at all. Now, the leaders of the March and the attendees would have to somehow translate that moment into action. They would have to change the attitudes, opinions and beliefs of people who did not want change, nor believed that the country needed it.

Although the event made an impression on people around the world, it was not immediately clear whether it would achieve its ultimate goal—passage of a civil rights bill. Following the March, the ten leaders met with President Kennedy. As the *New York Herald Tribune* reported, Kennedy ordered coffee, sandwiches, and cherry cobbler for his weary guests. Then he "sat down with them for a business session in the cabinet room. With him were Vice-President Johnson and Labor Secretary W. Willard Wirtz."

Later, House Speaker John W. McCormack told the group that the House would pass a civil rights bill that included two substantial (and controversial) additions to the President's original proposal: a section establishing a Fair Employment Practices Commission, and another giving the Attorney General broad authority to initiate suits to halt violations of constitutional rights.

Although Kennedy was impressed by the group's success in galvanizing tens of thousands of Americans in a peaceful demonstration, he was ever the pragmatic politician. For nearly an hour, Kennedy listened to the leaders make their case for the civil rights bill. Though he was moved by their well-chosen words, the President was also realistic that the civil rights bill, specifically the bill that the leaders wanted, stood little chance of passing.

And so, while he was a pleasant host, President Kennedy did not waver from the position that he had taken on the original bill. His ten guests, while polite, were steadfast in their position that the bill was flawed and needed to be amended. Throughout the conversation, the spirit of the March filled the room. Still, it appeared that the civil rights bill would face an uphill battle in Congress. Kennedy was certain it would be filibustered.

The Big Ten left the White House undaunted. There would be no time to bask in the glory of one of the most magnificent days of the twentieth century. They headed back to their communities, vowing to continue to register Negroes to vote, to protest inequities in education, labor, and housing.

Rustin suggested that if there was a filibuster over the civil rights bill, "one thousand demonstrators a day should descend upon Washington once the filibuster began, and constitute themselves into a 'People's Congress' to conduct their own hearings on the need for civil rights legislation." Rustin's idea might have taken hold if the nation and the world's attention had not been diverted by a shocking, senseless tragedy, once again, in Birmingham. On Sunday, September 15, 1963, a mere two weeks after the March, a bomb planted in the basement of the Sixteenth Street Baptist Church exploded, murdering four little girls: Denise McNair, Carole Robertson, Addie Mae Collins, and Cynthia Wesley.

The aftershocks of the bomb reverberated throughout the world. That four little girls could lose their lives in what should have been the safest place on earth gave everyone pause, and in that brief silence, a sense of clarity emerged. For a moment, support, however grudging, shifted toward passage of a civil rights bill.

On Friday, November 22, 1963, President Kennedy was assassinated in Dallas, Texas. Lyndon Baines Johnson became the President of the United States and vowed to follow through with Kennedy's civil rights agenda.

House opposition stalled the civil rights bill in the House Rules Committee. In the Senate, opponents attempted to talk it to death in a filibuster. In early 1964 supporters overcame the Rules Committee obstacle by threatening to send the bill to the floor without committee approval. The 75-day Senate filibuster ended through the floor leadership of Senator Hubert Humphrey of Minnesota, the support of President Lyndon Johnson, and the efforts of Senate Minority Leader Everett Dirksen of Illinois, who convinced Republicans to support the legislation.

The Civil Rights Act of 1964 outlawed segregation in businesses such as theaters, restaurants, and hotels. It banned discriminatory practices in employment and ended segregation in public places such as swimming pools, libraries, and public schools.

On July 2, 1964, one year after the meeting of the Big Six in New York City to develop a plan for the March on Washington for Jobs and Freedom, President Lyndon Johnson signed into law the Civil Rights Act of 1964.

POSTSCRIPT

Eugene Carson Blake was a noted Presbyterian ecumenist and pastor who championed peace and civil rights. Dismayed at the hundreds of divisions within the Protestant faith, Blake made the unprecedented proposal that the Protestant Episcopal Church and Northern Presbyterians both invite the Methodists and the United Church of Christ to form a new Christian Church, which would have created a denomination of 19 million members. Blake died in 1985.

James Farmer was founder of the Congress of Racial Equality (CORE), which he left in 1966. He joined the Nixon administration as Deputy Director of Health, Education and Welfare in 1969, but resigned eighteen months later. Born in 1920, he died on July 9, 1999. A noted professor at Mary Washington College, Farmer was awarded the Medal of Freedom by President Clinton in 1998.

Anna Arnold Hedgeman was born in 1899 and died in 1990. A founding member of the National Organization for Women, Hedgeman was a long-time activist for human and civil rights. Hedgeman served under Franklin Delano Roosevelt as executive director of his Fair Employment Practices Committee. She was instrumental in organizing the March on Washington.

Dr. Martin Luther King, Jr. won the Nobel Peace Prize in 1964 at age 35. He was the youngest man, second American, and third black man to win the prize. King led the Montgomery Improvement Association's successful bus boycott for more than a year, beginning in 1955. The former pastor of Dexter Avenue Baptist Church in Montgomery, Alabama, King was co-pastor (with his father) of Ebenezer Baptist Church from 1960 to 1968. Dr. King's non-violent method of protest transformed American activism. A dynamic orator and dedicated humanitarian, King was assassinated on April 4, 1968 while leading a sanitation workers' strike in Memphis, Tennessee. A national holiday in his honor was designated in 1986.

John Lewis, chair of the Southern NonViolent Coordinating Committee (SNCC), was the youngest speaker at the March on Washington. Lewis led a group of marchers across the Edmund Pettus Bridge in Selma, Alabama, on the infamous 1965 Bloody Sunday— one of two marches that resulted in the Voting Rights Act the same year. Elected to the Atlanta City Council in 1981, he won a seat in Congress (representing Georgia's fifth congressional district) in 1986, where he continues to serve. Lewis's memoir, *Walking With the Wind*, was a national bestseller. He was a 2001 recipient of the Profile in Courage Award for Lifetime Achievement.

Floyd McKissick was the second national director of the Congress of Racial Equality (CORE). An attorney and veteran of World War II, McKissick replaced James Foreman as head of CORE in 1966. He left the organization in 1968, and devoted many of his later years to Soul City, a planned integrated community in Warren, North Carolina that he envisioned as a community of 55,000 people. Born in 1922, McKissick died in 1989. Soul City was never realized.

Rabbi Joachim Prinz was born in 1902. Ordained as a rabbi at the Jewish Theological Seminary of Berlin in 1924, he became, in 1926, the youngest rabbi to serve Berlin's Jewish community. An outspoken critic of Nazism, Prinz left Germany. He arrived in the United States in 1937, where he was a popular lecturer, author and activist. He was president of the American Jewish Congress from 1958 to 1966. In April 1960, Prinz led a picket line to protest Woolworth's segregated lunch counters. Prinz died on September 30, 1988 at age 86.

Asa Philip Randolph was born on August 5, 1989. In 1925 he organized the Brotherhood of Sleeping Car Porters, one of the most powerful black labor unions ever. He was a vice-president of the AFL-CIO from 1955 to 1968. Randolph conceived the March on Washington. He received the Presidential Medal of Freedom in 1964 from President Lyndon Baines Johnson. Randolph died in 1979.

Walter P. Reuther rose to prominence as a leader of the United Auto Workers (UAW) infamous River Rouge Plant demonstration in 1937. Reuther was named president of the UAW in 1946. During his tenure he fought for a number of employee benefits, including health care, profit sharing, tuition reimbursement, and vacations. Born in 1907, Reuther died in a plane crash in 1970.

Bayard Rustin, who organized the March on Washington for Jobs and Freedom, was a committed pacifist and freedom fighter. Rustin planned the first freedom ride to the South, aptly titled "The Journey of Reconciliation." He introduced Gandhi's nonviolent techniques into the movement, which he taught to Dr. Martin Luther King, Jr. Raised a Quaker, Rustin was born in 1910. He died in 1987.

Roy Wilkins was a mighty force at the March on Washington, as he was in every aspect of the Civil Rights Movement. Wilkins succeeded W.E.B. DuBois as assistant executive secretary of the NAACP in 1931. In 1955 he accepted the position of executive secretary, and was executive director from 1965 until he retired in 1977. Wilkins, who was born in St. Paul, Minnesota, on August 30, 1901, died in 1981 in New York City. Upon his death, American flags were flown at half-mast on all government buildings.

Whitney M. Young led the National Urban League, the world's largest civil rights organization, for a decade, from 1961 to 1971. During that time, Young increased the number of Urban League's chapters from 60 to 98. He died on March 11, 1971 in Lagos, Nigeria, while attending a conference for black leaders.

SELECT BIBLIOGRAPHY
BOOKS AND MAGAZINE ARTICLES

Bennett, Lerone, Jr. "Masses were March heroes," *Ebony,* November 1963.

Blight, David W. *Race and Reunion: The Civil War in American Memory* (Belknap Press of Harvard University Press, 2001).

"Big Day—End And a Beginning," *Newsweek,* September 6, 1963.

Booker, Simeone. "What Negroes Can Expect from Kennedy," *Ebony,* September, 1960.

Branch, Taylor. *Parting the Waters: America in the King Years 1954-63* (Simon and Schuster, 1988).

"Civil Rights: The Awful Roar," *Time,* August 30 , 1963.

"Civil Rights: The March's Meaning," *Time,* September 6, 1963.

Clark Hine, Darlene and Kathleen Thompson. *A Shining Thread of Hope: The History of Black Women in America,* (Broadway Books, 1998).

Franklin, John Hope and Alfred A. Moss, Jr. *From Slavery to Freedom: A History of African Americans* (Alfred A. Knopf, 2000).

Garrow, David J. *Bearing the Cross: Martin Luther King, Jr. and the Southern Christian Leadership Conference* (William Morrow and Co., 1986).

Gentile, Thomas. *March on Washington, August 28, 1963* (New Day Publications,1983).

Haskins, James. *The March on Washington* (HarperCollins, 1993).

Hedgeman, Anna Arnold. *The Trumpet Sounds: A Memoir of Negro Leadership* (Holt, Rinehart and Winston, 1964).

Jones, Jacqueline. *American Work: Four Centuries of Black and White Labor* (W.W. Norton & Company, 1998).

Kasher, Steven. *The Civil Rights Movement: A Photographic History* (Abbeville Press, 1996).

Lewis, John with Michael D'Orso. *Walking With the Wind: A Memoir of the Movement* (Harcourt Brace & Company, 1998).

McWhorter, Diane. *Carry Me Home, Birmigham, Alabama: The Climactic Battle of the Civil Rights Revolution* (Simon and Schuster, 2001).

Olson, Lynne. *Freedom's Daughters: The Unsung Heroines of the Civil Rights Movement from 1830 to 1970* (Touchstone, 2001).

Pinderhughes, Dianne. "The Civil Rights Movement." In *Black Women in America: A Historical Encyclopedia.* Edited by Darlene Clark Hine, Rosalyn Terborg-Penn, and Elsa Barkley Brown (Carlson Publications, 1993).

Reeves, Thomas C. *A Question of Character: A Life of John F. Kennedy.* (Free Press, 1991).

Rowan, Carl. "Who Will Get the Negro Vote?", *Ebony,* May 1960.

Stewart, Jeffrey C. *1001 Things Everyone Should Know About African American History* (Doubleday, 1996).

NEWSPAPER ARTICLES
(IN CHRONOLOGICAL ORDER)

Randolph, A. Philip "March of 10,000 Workers on Capital Called Way to Get Jobs." *Washington Afro American,* March 15, 1941.

Randolph, A. Philip "Why F.D.R. Won't End Defense Jim Crow. *Richmond Afro American,* April 12, 1941.

"10,000 Will March on D.C." *The Washington Afro American,* May 10, 1941.

"Group Making July 1 Plans," *The New York Amsterdam Star News.* May 24, 1941.

"Roosevelt Issues Executive Order," *The New York Amsterdam Star News.* June 28, 1941.

"D.C. March for Jobs Called Off," *Washington Afro American.* June 28, 1941.

Wilkins, Roy. "Watchtower," *New York Amsterdam Star News,* June 28, 1941.

"Did a Phone Call Elect Kennedy President?" *Negro Digest,* November, 1961.

Rasa Gustaitis, "March Headquarters Bustle with Confusion," *The Washington Post,* August 28, 1963.

John Maffre, "March Stirs Conscience of the World," *The Washington Post,* August 29, 1963.

"Negroes' Leader A Man of Dignity," *The New York Times,* August 29, 1963.

James Reston, "I Have a Dream...," *The New York Times,* August 29, 1963.

Gay Talese, "The Talk of Harlem," *The New York Times,* August 29, 1963.

August 28, 1963: One of the greatest days of the 20th century.

PHOTOGRAPHY CREDITS

Cover Credits:

Front cover photograph: © Flip Schulke/CORBIS

Front cover inset, spine and back cover photograph: AP/Wide World Photos

Interior Credits

© Steve Schapiro/STOCKPHOTO.COM: p. 5 (original in color)

© Ivan Massar/ STOCKPHOTO.COM: p. 10 (detail)

© Flip Schulke/CORBIS: pp. 20, 40 (original in color), 58 (detail)

© Fred Ward/STOCKPHOTO.COM: pp. 30, 98, 102, 114 (detail)

© Bob Adelman/Magnum Photos: pp. 54, 138 (detail)

© Leonard Freed/Magnum Photos: p. 74

© Bettmann/CORBIS: p. 84 (detail)

© Hulton-Deutsch Collection/CORBIS: p. 118 (detail)

© Robert W. Kelley/TimePix: p. 156